WAKE UP
and
DREAM

"Pat's life is an outstanding example of the dream principle in action. This wonderful book was recommended to us by some of our most respected dreamers, and we now know why. We continue to apply these same principles in our lives to achieve a measure of significance and we encourage others to apply Pat's formula and change their world for the better."

JIM AND NANCY DORNAN

"Pat Mesiti is a dreamer but he also makes other people's dreams come true. I highly recommend this book as an inspirational tool for success.

Pat Mesiti has lived the essence of this volume ... hold on to your dream and never quit. Without equivocation I commend Pat's words of wisdom to you."

DR EDWIN LOUIS COLE

"Nothing more vividly illustrates the power of a dream than stories like Pat Mesiti's own life. I have worked alongside Pat for ten years and have witnessed first-hand his rise from the streets of Bankstown in Sydney, Australia to a position of international impact. Through his books, business conferences and work with Youth Alive, this gifted communicator is impacting hundreds and thousands of people each year–and the dangerous part is ... he's still dreaming new dreams!"

BRIAN HOUSTON

"Without a dream, life is meaningless. For every dreamer there is a dream "maker" or a dream "breaker". Pat Mesiti is a dream maker..."

DAVE ROEVER

Wake Up and Dream
Copyright © 1994 Pat Mesiti Ministries
Educational, Motivational

ISBN 0 646 19211 6

Typeset by The Amazing Hat Company
PO Box 198
Killarney Vale NSW 2261
Telephone: (043) 881986

Cover design by CPGD
4 Marguerite Crescent
West Pennant Hills, NSW 2125

Printed in Australia by
Pirie Printers
140 Gladstone Street
(P O Box 438) Fyshwick
Canberra ACT 2609

This book is dedicated to all my
Youth Alive friends and to the kids
that make Youth Alive what it is.

Thank you for being part of the
world's answer rather than
part of its problems.

You're the Best!

Keep dreaming that we can
change the world.

Contents

To the Dream Builders

Many people dream alone, but few dreams ever come to fruition without the contribution of committed people giving freely of their time and talents. Dream builders, are those special people who take the seeds of vision and turn them into a living fruitful reality.

I am forever grateful to all the dream builders who have helped me along the way.

I would like to thank Craig Hingston for his assistance and great patience and for taking my spoken messages, words and scribbled notes and making them not only sound legible, but actually intelligent. Craig–you are unique and so consistently positive, thanks for all the effort, mate.

I would also like to thank Paul and Sallie-Ann Macklin for helping me finalise this project and Owen Salter for the finishing touches.

All my staff at Youth Alive: Kylie Taylor, my able assistant–for your hard work and for being there beyond the call of duty; Lyn Ollis–for making events happen the way they do; Paul Innuzzellli–keep writing those songs and keep "Jumping to the Jam"; Michael Cowdroy–for following up the kids when everyone else forgets about them.

To my board: Michael Murphy, Nabi Saleh, Leigh Howard-Smith, Kevin Brett, Jonathon de Jong and Steven Crouch–for all of their discernment, insight, wisdom and support.

To my best friend, Brian Houston: Keep serving the Lord with gladness. Brian, you're an inspiring leader and a great friend, thanks for helping me make my dreams come true.

Last but not least, **to my wife Liz, for her strength, encouragement, support, love and commitment. You're the best thing that ever happened to a Bankstown boy!!!**

To my daughters, Rebecca and Chantelle: Dad loves you so much–words can't express how much I miss you when I'm away. The future's in your hands and I know it's in good hands. You're the best kids in the world.

If I have forgotten to mention you in my acknowledgements please fill in your name here...

Foreword

Curiosity was killing me. It seemed every switched on young person with whom I came in contact raved about him. I resolved to track this human phenomenon down. My search led me to the city of Sydney where a massive event was being staged.

My effort in finding an available car park was further frustrated by having to navigate my way through what seemed to be a bus convention. Out of those buses poured thousands of young people charged with excitement for what lay moments ahead–YOUTH ALIVE. The dream, the vision, the reality of one man, Pat Mesiti.

Wanting to get a close up view of this guy, I proceeded towards the front of the auditorium, only to be held back by six thousand young people standing toe to heel.

Some people walk on to stage–that's not Pat's style–he *explodes* on to stage. His presence was like a spark to a keg of sun-dried gunpowder. From that moment, the auditorium vibrated under the intensity of young people enraptured and in their element.

Pat's mission that night, as with his whole life, was to impart hope and inspire his listeners to a life of greatness. He succeeded ... and continues to succeed.

Hoping one day the privilege would be mine of meeting this man, I have had one of my dreams come true–I have become his friend. Pat has inspired me, as well as people of every age, from the arena of adolescence, the world of business and the conventions of successful leaders. He will inspire you, too.

Anyone who aspires to a life of greatness will benefit from reaching out and grabbing the encouragement and principles Pat imparts in his book *Wake Up and Dream.*

Wes Beavis

Introduction

You've picked up this book and there's a reason for it.

You've shown the first quality of being a dreamer. You're dissatisfied with the way things are as you look around and you want to see some changes, some improvements. You're not content with the status quo.

After all, why shouldn't you have a better lifestyle, a better self-image, a better community ... and a better world? And why shouldn't you and everybody else enjoy a better future full of hope?

I remember a while ago I was talking to a group of people, radical thinkers who love to come up with exciting ideas and plans. We were sharing our thoughts about the future and getting each other motivated when a guy who was really cynical said, "Mesiti, you're nothing but a dreamer." He meant it as a slur, but I took it as a compliment. You see, I've got a confession to make: I am a dreamer!

The way I see it, why not have the kind of home life you dream about? Why not be surrounded by kind, loving people who have a genuine concern for you and your future? And why not live in a society that is safe?

Why not become a successful business person? Why not become the best athlete this nation has ever seen? Why not enjoy prosperity and rewards which today are just storybook fantasies in your mind?

This book asks you "Why not?"- and the answer is "There's no reason why not." It all boils down to one thing. Having a dream. Being a dreamer.

One day in the future you might be asked if you were part of the dramatic, positive changes of your world. If you would like to be the sort of person who can reply "I wasn't just part of them–I was making them!", then this book is for you!

Part One

WAKE UP!

Chapter One

YOU CAN CHANGE
YOUR WORLD

Ibelieve the "average" person can change their world. In this book, which is the result of many years of learning and of good and bad experiences in my life, I will challenge you to become a dreamer. And more than that, to become an achiever.

I don't care how average you think you are, how ordinary you feel, or how ineffective you might consider your life. I'm going to show you that simply by taking what you have, and who you are right now, you can become a radically better person. And you can make a mark on your world.

How do I know? Because I was an average kid. I've gone from being a so-called misfit at school, getting bad grades and being beaten by my drunk parents, to overseeing an international ministry aimed at helping young people.

I'll start off by giving you an overview of my childhood and you'll see that even when life's against you, you can still get out there and make a go of it.

My Story

I was born into a working class Italian family, at Bankstown, a strong ethnic suburban area in Sydney, Australia. This is an older part of the city, near the international airport and industrial areas, with a lot of crowded houses and streets full of old cars.

My father was a factory worker and my mother, who was illiterate, was at home. To make this worse they were both alcoholics. I went to Catholic primary and high schools where the only things I really excelled in were Rugby League, boxing and starting fights!

One of my teachers in high school (I'll never forget this; it's incredible how a single statement can stick in your mind all your life) told me that I'd never amount to anything and I'd most likely end up in jail. Or dead.

I had a very violent home life. My father was continually drunk. He would shout and throw things around the house, use abusive language, beat my mother and take out his anger on me too. Not only this, but every day when I came home from school my mother was falling around drunk–although she never admitted to having a drinking problem.

I remember being made to stand outside bars waiting for Dad to come out after his drinking binges. I was about seven years old and had to carry the bags of shopping, help him onto the bus and try to explain to the passengers that he was staggering because he wasn't feeling well. Can you imagine being that little boy, feeling the ridicule of people as they laughed at you and your Dad? They knew and I knew exactly what they were thinking: the man's a drunk.

Growing up with that kind of humiliation robs you of security and a sense of self-respect. Not only that–it makes you very angry. At your parents, your world and yourself.

Another memory I have is of putting up a screen door when I was a kid. I'd just finished, after taking all day to do it, when Dad and my elder brother got into a big argument and crashed right through it. I can still picture myself standing there in shock, holding the screwdriver, as the two adults propelled themselves through my work of art. I vowed then I would never pick up a screwdriver again.

By the time I was in my teens the violence and drinking at home had worsened. High school is tough enough without having alcoholism rule your home. This kind of upbringing creates a lot of negative attitudes, and believe me, I had plenty. I reacted by becoming angry and violent. Some people said it was a stage I was going through. Others just pointed to my family and blamed them. I wanted to do well at school but couldn't do my homework because I was too busy trying to keep my father from killing my mother, my brother from killing my father, and me from killing me. This meant I was failing my exams and the teachers gave me a hard time. Some of them thought I was lazy, but I couldn't tell them the truth.

---

*It's not what happens
or has happened to us
in life that counts.
It's how we respond
to what happens
that's important.*

I had every reason to accept this as "my lot in life". But I saw what was going on around me and had a pretty good idea of where it was going to take me. That caused me to make the decision to "break out".

I believe this is the first step to changing your life. You have to come to the realisation that despite the fact that your parents are alcoholics or career-conscious without quality time for you, despite the fact that you are growing up on "the wrong side of the tracks", despite the fact that you're hopeless at school, you can decide to WAKE UP!

Snap out of it! Enough is enough. Decide what kind of future you want.

Created For Greatness

Ever since I was at high school I've had a dream to do something effective with young people. I love their vitality, their free-thinking, their boldness and adventurous spirit. As I grew older I saw that life appeared to be knocking the stuffing out of a lot of them. They were losing hope for the future, and this made me even more determined to make a positive impact.

My teenage observations became an all-consuming desire which has now developed into an international ministry, presenting a message of hope and offering positive role models to hundreds of thousands of primary and high school kids, school leavers, university students and business people.

Why did I have this dream to reach out to the next generation? Was it because I had such a rough upbringing and I wanted to make sure others didn't have to go through that? This probably has something to do with it. But the bottom line was that I didn't want to become a victim of my circumstances.

I grasped early on that we are created for greatness. We are incredibly creative, emotive beings. Something stirred inside me. It caused me to "wake up" from the slumber of being conditioned to accept the status quo. And "waking up" is the first step towards reaching your dreams.

I am continually relating to young people, teenagers, business people and clergymen in all parts of the world. No matter where I go, I see people missing out on reaching their full potential in life because they don't have a reason to move ahead and achieve. This led me to put my experiences and positive material together in this book.

I hope it will help people everywhere to rise up and change themselves and their world.

Chapter Two

HOW MANY MORE SLEEPS UNTIL WE WAKE UP?

I t's a tragic indictment on our society but many people are asleep 24 hours a day. There's no light on inside.

They're the "walking dead". Why haven't they woken up yet? There are a number of reasons.

People are lulled to sleep by apathy, complacency, compromise, procrastination and a sense that everything will work out in the end. They don't have a purpose in life and aren't committed to anything. Maybe they are afraid of waking up and prefer to stay wrapped up in their nice warm comfort zone.

It is said that our Western world is in a state of apathy, ruled by a "who cares?" attitude to life. People live with a "cruising mentality", doing enough to get by and no more. They say, "Don't rock the boat, it'll all work out in the end". All they end up doing is settling for less than the best.

Apathy is one of the greatest killers of success. It kills motivation, vision and destiny.

Apathy has to be the ugliest word in the English language. Apathetic people make excuses. They reason away why they aren't getting ahead in life or achieving. One common excuse is that they're waiting for the "big break", when all circumstances will be perfect.

The reality is, if you're asleep to opportunities, you'll miss all the breaks that come your way.

I like what Og Mandino says: "Be prepared to capitalise on the next opportunity that presents itself or, better still, to make your own opportunities."

Stretch and Grow

Why have a dream? One reason is to develop yourself, for personal growth. A vision for your future will cause you to stretch further and develop the necessary skills to accomplish it.

During the early days of raising up the Youth Alive movement, I was mainly focussed on addressing youth issues and providing young people with relevant, contemporary events. As the organisation grew, I found that I also had to become skilled in managing people, concerts, finances and promotions. I didn't learn these skills overnight. Some of them took me a while to grasp, and I remember that was a very stretching time. But the experience was vital and through it I grew.

Here's a great quote I picked up: "Always dream and shoot higher than you know you can reach. Don't bother just to be better than your contemporaries or predecessors, try to be better than yourself." Without a vision you will stay at the level of mediocrity.

Be prepared to capitalise on the next opportunity that presents itself or, better still, to make your own opportunities.

Dreamers tend to shoot higher than what has already been achieved. At every Olympic Games records are broken. Those athletes are not content to live within their old time or those set by someone else. Their goal is not just to win a gold medal, but to join that class of elite people who go beyond themselves. They want to be known as someone who dared to believe.

When the world's number one runner sprints down the track, he is in competition with himself. He wants to beat his current best time and set a new one. He is definitely awake!

Enjoy the Trip

Life should be fun. You should be enjoying yourself each day. When you're in pursuit of a dream, realising your goals each step of the way, you experience immense satisfaction and personal achievement. It's about time we turned off the snooze button of life, woke up and began to dream.

The 1980s and 1990s have seen so many people lose hope. I've read about thousands of businesses going under. Family breakdowns are increasing. There are more homeless kids on the streets than before. Violence is escalating. Teenage suicide, one of the signs of helplessness in our younger generation, keeps rising. It's so tragic. So many wasted lives.

To have a dream is to have hope, to believe in a better tomorrow. That in itself is worth dreaming.

I had this brought home to me when I was speaking at a youth camp at the same time the Gulf War broke out. The kids went quiet. Rather than race around outside on the football field and tennis courts, or go swimming at the beach like normal hyped-up-on-Koolaid type teenagers, they sat mesmerised in front of a TV as the world blew itself to pieces. Their faces were full of fear.

As I spoke to them I realised that here were

young people with no hope for tomorrow. Scared of Armageddon, fearful for their destinies and relationships, they were wondering if this could be the end.

By the end of the week, these same fear-struck kids were changed into what we could call "world changers". They were encouraged to become dreamers and believe they could create a better tomorrow. They had taken part in a battle of their own–a fight against negativity and lost hope. Their Gulf War had been against the gulf between fear and the future. And they had won.

The young people went home hopeful rather than hapless, sensing destiny rather than defeat. They had become victors rather than victims. Today some of those world changers are in foreign nations working in missionary service and others are leaders in business and community service. They woke up.

It Won't Happen Overnight

One of the greatest satisfactions of life is not just to achieve a goal but to pursue it. I have heard success described as the pursuit of a worthwhile dream. The pursuit should be as enjoyable as the ultimate reward. I know that in the time it has taken us to build Youth Alive from impacting 350 young people to multiple thousands I have enjoyed the journey. Well, most of it!

I like to read about other dreamers and how they "woke up", "birthed" a dream and achieved it. Three that come to mind are an athlete, a musician and a poor single mother, all of whom expressed a deep satisfaction at pursuing their dreams.

The young speed skater, Eric Heiden, was a great crowd pleaser at the 1980 Winter Olympic Games in Lake Placid, New York, and won a number of gold medals but he said that throughout his training he had a greater desire. The Olympic wins were simply a step along the way to achieving a greater dream: to be a successful surgeon like his father.

Fritz Chrysler, the great violinist, was once approached backstage by an enthusiastic fan who said, "Mr Chrysler, I'd give my life to play as you do."

He replied, "Madam, I did." His dream had become his life.

Then there's the story of Romana Banuelos. What a dreamer. She got married in Mexico at 16 but before she'd left her teens she was a divorcee with two children. Determined to provide a life of dignity and pride for her sons, she packed all her worldly possessions in a small bundle and crossed the rugged border country into Texas.

Romana's first job was working in a laundry for a dollar a day. With seven dollars in her pocket she moved to Los Angeles and took on odd jobs whenever she could. Gradually, month by month, she saved until she had $400 which she used to buy a small tortilla shop with her aunt. That one shop became two, five, ten, then Romana's Mexican Food Products–the largest Mexican wholesale food concern in the nation! It grew from a two–person operation to employing hundreds.

"I know of no more encouraging fact than the unquestionable ability of man to elevate his life by conscious endeavour."
Henry David Thoreau

Having achieved financial security for her sons, Romana turned her attention to her fellow Mexican–Americans. She decided to set up a bank to serve that community. The Pan–American National Bank in East L.A. began in a small caravan. Despite many challenges, it grew to the level where its resources are valued at over twenty million dollars.

More was to come for this courageous dreamer. Romana moved on from banking to become the 34th Treasurer of the United States of America! Her signature appears on billions of dollars of US currency.

From a young single mum earning a dollar a day to one of the most powerful figures in the most powerful nation on earth. That's the power of a dream.

Michael Beer, author of *The Joy Of Winning*, puts it well: "One of the winner's consistent characteristics is a powerful all-consuming sense of destination. He knows where he is going."

Perish the Thought

There is a biblical proverb which says without a vision people will perish. That word "perish" means you are doomed to defeat, scattered and put to confusion. What a terrible state to be in.

Vision clears confusion and gives you focus. It destroys a defeatist attitude and causes you to be locked on to where you are going rather than scattered and distraught.

Dreams Change Lives

You've read this far yet you might still be thinking: What will a dream do for me? How can it change me?

In a nutshell: dreams will make you. They will create your character, your attitudes. Build you up. Make you a better you–unless you like the you that you are and don't want a New Improved Version!.

"This is the true joy in life, being used for a purpose recognised by yourself as a mighty one.
Being a force of nature instead of a feverish, selfish little clod of ailments and grievances complaining that the world will not devote itself to making you happy."
Bernard Shaw

Along the way you'll get to know your strengths and weaknesses. I wasn't a confident person in the early days. I didn't feel secure in what I was doing; in fact, it was quite nerve-wracking sometimes. I was so sick with anxiety before my first rally that I had to go home ill and get a friend to stand in for me!

Today, years of speaking, leading rallies and helping people of all ages and backgrounds has given me the confidence to tackle bigger dreams.

Dreaming makes you a risk-taker. It challenges you to step out, stop playing it safe, move out of your comfort zone and dare to believe. It gives you real purpose.

SUMMARY

1. Determine to wake up
2. Declare war on apathy, compromise and procrastination
3. Consider your purpose in life
4. Analyse your abilities and talents

You need dreams in your life to:
1. Better yourself
2. Give your life purpose and direction
3. Not be controlled by outside circumstances
4. Get out of mere existence mode
5. Get more enjoyment out of life
6. Affect other people's lives for the better

Chapter Three

THE BIRTH OF A DREAMER

Once you've determined to wake up, you need to create your dream. I've noticed that my dreams have followed the same path as the life of a human being. Before a baby is born it must develop through several stages, and the birth of a dream is no different. It all begins with conception, followed by formation, incubation and birth.

I'm asked to address young people and business people the world over. Doors of opportunity have opened for me in the most unlikely places. As I look back over my life I can clearly see how I conceived a dream, gave it form, helped it grow, then saw it birthed.

In much the same way as the egg and sperm bare no resemblance to the fully formed human baby, my early dream was a long way from what I'm doing today. It all began when I was 16 years old. I was sitting in what they called a 'youth rally' and the only word that I could think to describe it was boring. This event was so boring that boring people called it boring. As a matter of fact, not only was it boring, it lacked any sense of excellence or professionalism.

The choir was (you guessed it) boring. The music was (that's right) boring. Add awful to that as well. The speaker had no reason to be there because he was . . . boring. As I suffered that evening from noise pollution I felt an inner voice–that still, small voice of destiny–say, "Son, you'll take over this one day." I said, "Good. The first thing I'm going to do is fire the choir, and I'm going to change its name."

A Seed Had Been Planted.

I began sharing my desire to get involved. I started to get a burning ambition for the youth rallies. The leadership wanted to invite a guy from another country to run it, but I told them, "He won't come, he doesn't have a vision for it. It's my dream!"

Some time after I'd endured that woefully boring meeting I was approached to take over and to make our young people nice. I said, "Forget it. I'll gladly take over, but I want to make them radicals, not nice."

World changers and dreamers aren't always nice. They're compassionate, but not necessarily nice. They're loving, yet will dare to effectively pioneer and pave the way for others. They run the risk of often being misunder-stood–except by other dreamers. You might feel that no-one understands your dream. You're probably right. Don't expect people to–even your closest friends or family members. Keep dreaming and pave the way for others, and they will follow.

So it was that I entered this group of apathetic, indifferent teenagers who have now become compassionate-and-daring, effective-yet-loving, sometimes-misunderstood pioneers. And it was the start of the most exciting adventure I could ever imagine.

From Small Beginnings

There I was with a small group of people and an idea. I had the belief that one day I would be impacting and changing the lives of thousands. The organisation we called Youth Alive began with about 350 young people. It started as a seed thought and has developed into one of the greatest youth movements in the world. It has not only given me a sense of identity and achievement but also helped countless others make positive changes in their lives.

The Dream Conceived

You might think that the "conception" of my dream to work with young people began when I decided to take over the youth rallies. However, as I look back over my younger days I can see a significant incident which really sparked it off for me.

I didn't do that well at school, as I've mentioned, and the teachers said I was a no-hoper. All except one, my English teacher. He was a former pilot and the school's boxing coach.

I was involved in boxing and really wanted to compete in a big championship. Everyone ridiculed me (and if you've seen me in the flesh you'll know why)–except for my English teacher. He basically said, "Mesiti, you can be anything you want."

It's that attitude I still believe in today.

I believe that small incident where someone believed in me was the "conception". It led to the desire to want to help young people.

The Dream Nourished

I nourished that dream by getting involved in youth activities, mixing with young people, learning to understand them, finding out what they wanted. As a result, I was at the right place at the right time for the "birth".

I love the movie *Field Of Dreams*. What a

concept! The central character, played by Kevin Costner, is a mid-western corn farmer in the United States who hears a voice over and over saying, "If you build it, he will come." Puzzled at first, Costner soon finds out he is meant to clear some of his land–his liveli-hood–and build a baseball field in a cornfield. The reason for it is not immediately known, but it becomes more and more obvious as the movie goes on.

Everything starts and finishes with a dream.

The farmer is ridiculed and criticised, threatens his own meagre finances by reducing the size of his crop. But he sticks to the dream. With an all-consuming passion he is driven to attempt the unnatural, the extra-ordinary. He doesn't have all of the facts, but he has passion, a sense of purpose.

One day, as the farmer gazes out over his empty baseball diamond, ghost-characters from previous generations magically appear to play ball. The only people who can see the ghosts in action are the farmer, his wife and his little daughter–the dreamers. The wife's brother, a real cynic, ridicules them for staring into space until at the end of the story he too is able to see. Dreams are not immediately noticeable but given time they will materialise. Other characters from the present make their way to the cornfield and realise their life dreams through the ghostly game. There is a doctor who has given up the big time in baseball to pursue medicine, a 1960s baseball writer who wants to return to the innocence of a bygone era and the farmer who wants to be re-united with the father he's found it hard to relate to. He "meets" him on that field and they play ball together.

Everything starts and finishes with a dream. The dream makes you, and you make the dream. Your identity as a person and your actions, thoughts, ideas and behaviour are inseparable.

The Birth

Was the birth of Youth Alive painful? You bet! What stood in my way was old thinking, cultural irrelevancy and people who were generally about twenty years behind the times.

Looking back I thank God for every obstacle and every lesson learnt, because today the dream I had of filling the largest auditoriums with people who hadn't fried their brains with acid, is coming true. Actually, the kids who do destroy their bodies with drugs also come to our meetings. The destitute and abused, broken and poor, afflicted and addicted come and find help, counsel and freedom. It's for these people that the dream was created. I see them as they can become, not as they are.

I recall a young man named Fred. When he came to us he had been thrown out of home. He was trying to put himself through school whilst being addicted to substances such as marijuana and other drugs. He could barely talk straight, let alone think straight.

Through faith and a sense of destiny, this reject in the eyes of many has become a very successful businessman. In a few years he has built a million dollar business, and he now supports the work that rescued him from his nightmare life of misery.

That's what can happen when a dream is conceived, nurtured and brought to birth.

Pain and Sacrifice

Growth spurts are painful too. I will never forget the challenges we faced as we outgrew smaller venues and had to graduate to the "big time"–from a 2,500-seat auditorium to a 5,500-seat building, to a modern 7,000-seat sports centre and then to the biggest indoor entertainment venue available to us. Each transition stretched us and forced us to change the ways we ran Youth Alive–for the better.

As well as the pain there is sacrifice. There is a cost to having children; I know, I have two. For parents it can mean "adjustments" to the shape of their body, less sleep, rearranging lifestyle and priorities, and less freedom. A worthwhile dream or purpose in life will also cost you something. Before starting out in pursuit of your dream, you need to understand this.

I remember once being approached by a person who asked me to get involved in a business scheme.

"Will it take time?" I asked.

"No, of course not."

"Will it cost me personally?"

"No."

"Then it's not worth getting involved in," I replied.

Personal cost is something that never stops. In 1993, I was offered an opportunity to speak at an event where I would be well paid for my services. However, I had also been asked to speak to ghetto kids in New York. On the one hand was a lucrative payment; on the other, all the risks associated with living in the ghetto and staying in a run-down apartment with rats.

One of my friends said, "Cancel the trip to New York and take the lucrative engagement. Those street kids and crack kids will be there next week." I replied, "Maybe they won't," and off I went.

I had to consider my original motives and go back to the days when I conceived and birthed my dream.

There is something far greater than money–it is purpose.

---

*There is something
far greater than money...
it is purpose.*

Purpose And Priorities

Recently I got the chance to speak at a big event in another country. For years I had desired to go there. I burned with excitement. Then came the news–my father was diagnosed with cancer and was dying.

Here was another choice: prominence versus significance. Taking the speaking engagement would cause me to become a lot more well known. Staying with my father and helping him through possibly the last days of his life would be significant.

I thought, "The speaking opportunities will come and go, but I've only got one Dad." I stayed home and my father pulled through (I nickname him Lazarus now!). The opportunity to speak in that country came again. It was a case of knowing my priorities, of knowing what came first. But such experiences are painful all the same.

Newborn–Unknown Ability

When a child is born we have no way of knowing what abilities it will have or who it will become. The great musician Bob Dylan was an unknown Robert Zimmerman until he became BOB DYLAN. Elvis was just plain old Elvis Presley until he became ELVIS PRESLEY.

---

*Begin to be now
what you will be
tomorrow.*

When we begin on our journey towards our dream we have no knowledge of all our talents and abilities. But that must not stop us from starting out. There's an old proverb by Saint Jerome which says, "Begin to be now what you will be hereafter." And, even if you consider yourself to be someone lacking in ability, consider the words of Kenneth Hildebrand: "People with ordinary talents often achieve more than those with greater physical and intellectual endowments because they work harder with what they have. "

A little while ago I had a firsthand experience of seeing someone wake up and birth a dream. It happened when I was asked to speak at a roller-skating rink. That night I had planned to relax with a good book and plenty of Italian coffee, but I was interrupted by the phone and a request to speak to 400 teenagers at the rink.

When I drove up I could hear music blaring. It sounded like cats screaming in pain, explosions and growling voices like *Friday 13th*'s Freddy Kruger! The room was filled with cigarette and dope smoke. There were young people standing around looking bored with their tattoos, scars, teeth knocked out, and hair past their waists. And these were just the females!

I thought to myself: "Either they're going to kill me or I'm going to motivate them." Needless to say, I won. That's why I'm writing this book.

At the end of the night, with the kids sitting there crying and laughing, I challenged them about their lives, their futures and their relationship with their Creator. A young man came up to me with baggy eyes and a depressed look and said, "Man, I've got a problem."

"You look like a problem," I replied.

"I do drugs," he explained.

"Why do you do drugs?"

"'Cause."

"'Cause why?"

"I don't know."

"How are things at home?"

"Great."

"Have you got girlfriend troubles?"

"No."

As I looked into his eyes I saw one of the most frightening things I've ever seen. No, not a gremlin. What I saw was a young man without purpose or destiny.

I said, "The reason you do drugs is because you've got *no reason not to do drugs, and you have no reason for living.*" He burst into tears, and for the next little while we talked and prayed and dreamed and shared.

This young man decided to break out of his peer group. He found a purpose worth pursuing, gave up the drugs, started improving his grades at school and is now preparing for a great life in the business world. He was in sleep mode, then he was woken up by a dream.

It's stories like this which give me the greatest satisfaction in life. In finding his dream he was leading me to mine.

My greatest desire in putting my thoughts on paper is that you too will become a dreamer. My hope is that you will determine to give your life real purpose; that you will consider what you want to achieve and set goals; that you will write down your goals and pursue them in a balanced, mature manner. And in doing so I hope that you will become successful and prosperous–which is exactly what God wants for your life.

I dare you to become a dreamer!

SUMMARY

1. Don't wait for a "big break"; conceive your dream now
2. Nurture your dream through its "pregnancy"
3. Be willing to endure the pain of "birthing" your dream
4. Allow your dream to grow in stages
5. Think big–your "infant" dream will bear little resemblance to your "mature" dream.

Part Two

ANATOMY OF A DREAMER

Chapter Four

THE HEAD AND MIND

Conceive and believe the dream

W e're born with a head, two arms, two legs, two eyes, a nose and so on. As my thoughts and experiences poured out in preparation for this book, I noticed they fitted into a structure–something like the parts that make up the human body.

Thinking about them in this way helps me interpret and understand what I've learned. A body without legs won't run far. A body without a mind can't operate. In the same way, a dreamer without a work ethic or without imagination and planning won't get ahead. A body needs all of its components to function as it was intended. A dreamer needs all of the characteristics to move ahead.

How have I identified these characteristic's? I've seen them in the lives of other people who are pursuing their dreams. Not just the well-known personalities you read about in motivational books, but also the unheard of people like those I meet in my travels. They are my inspiration.

It's a big list but don't be daunted by it. In the same way that a dream is conceived and born, it must also go through "infancy" to "childhood" to "adulthood". We don't expect kids to make adult decisions and run a home or a business.

If you're in the early stages of thinking about your life purpose and where you'd like to go, don't think you have to achieve it by next month. Allow yourself to know what qualities are important, then be patient with yourself and help them mature bit by bit as you move ahead.

Here we go, then. We start at the top–with the head.

THE HEAD

The head is one of the heaviest parts of the body and the most important. It's the nerve centre. Four of our five senses (sight, hearing, smell and taste) are located here.

In our society a lot of importance is placed on the exterior of the head, especially the face. Yet it's the inside–your mind, dreams, destiny and character– which are of most importance.

Life can be like that too–a facade. Some people spend a lot of time and money taking care of their outward appearance, but forget the inner things.

The superficiality of our world makes it empty and shallow. Like the empty "I love you", a young man tells his girlfriend only to get what he wants. The loyal, hard working staff member deserves more recognition than a pat "Thanks", from their employer. Or the superficiality of a parent who believes in their family but continues indulging in illicit affairs.

A dreamer goes beyond the face of things and has a good head on his or her shoulders.

Foundation, substance, moral values, character–these are what lie behind a dreamer. True dreamers are deep yet fun-loving, content yet dissatisfied, mature yet with a yearning to grow.

Dreamers are not impressed by the trappings of superficial people. They desire reality. They seek to live an effective life which can impact their world.

Pretend Success Or Inner Wealth?

We live in a society where a lovely home in a nice leafy suburb, luxury cars in the driveway, kids at private schools, holidays overseas, and designer clothes all say, "I'm a success." Yet the whole lot might be propped up with a dozen credit cards on the limit, personal loans or lease contracts and shaky finances. Is that success?

Inner Wealth

Dreamers realise that true wealth comes from within, from qualities such as character, integrity, honesty, righteousness, truth, a sense of justice and fair play, and balance (achieving excellence in all areas of life, not just one or two).

Someone displaying these qualities who lives in a typical middle-class suburb and drives a tidy yet average family sedan has a better foundation to work from than a "keep up with the Joneses at all costs" person.

It's not the house you live in that counts, it's the home you create inside the house. It's not the car you drive that gives you identity and worth but the inner character of the driver.

What you are behind the face is more important than what you look like outside.

THE MIND

The mind of a dreamer is in forward–or positive–gear. A visionary is a creative thinker, diligent, persevering, coming up with solutions and not dwelling on problems.

"As a man thinks so he is", says the Bible. In other words, you are what you think. Your mind affects your behaviour.

One of the most undervalued parts of the mind is our imagination. It's also one of the most misused.

Everything that exists–cars, planes, houses, even chairs and coffee mugs–began as an image in someone's imagination.

---

*What the mind can
conceive and believe
it can achieve.*

You can imagine your future, your successes and your achievements right inside your head. Over and over again. Just like a full colour Surround Sound movie, except there's no popcorn or Coke.

Set your mind to conceive and believe.

Imagine Your Success

Think about it: you're only limited by the boundaries you place on yourself. Dream about contentedness, about the house you want to live in, about the organisations or causes you want to support. Dream about the career you want to pursue and the effect it will have. Dream about having a loving, supporting family. The power of the human mind and our capacity to dream is God-created and beyond our comprehension.

Do you want to build a home to your own floor plans? Imagine it. Do you want to travel interstate or overseas on holidays? Imagine it. Do you want to be managing director or number one sales executive? Imagine it. Do you want to write a cheque to a charity for $10,000? Imagine it. Do you want to write a cheque to Youth Alive for $10,000? I'd be glad to accept it!

Don't limit yourself,
dream big dreams,
tackle great challenges.

When Youth Alive rallies drew crowds of several hundred people I was imagining 1,000 in front of me. When we had 1,000 people I could "see" 2,000 in my mind. I used to go to the biggest auditorium for rock concerts in my city and imagine myself on stage. People would ask me how we were going to fill it and I'd reply, "We've already been there–in my mind." Today, I imagine huge crowds filling the largest sporting venue in the country.

Find A Quiet Place

It's good to find a quiet place where you can relax and let your mind go. I do a lot of my imagining when I'm driving the car (don't worry, I keep my eyes open!). This is not some weird mind game where you lose control. Rather it is controlled thinking.

The biblical proverb is correct: "*As a man thinks so he is.*" My manager, Paul, imagines himself speaking to groups of people. He prepares his message in his mind, sees the people responding and laughing at the right time. Then when he delivers his message he sees it happen.

I've read about a basketball team in the US which imagined shooting baskets whilst other players trained regularly each day. After a week they all got together to compare their improvement. The ones who saw themselves getting baskets and slam dunks improved the same as the ones who trained!

Your imagination is very powerful. It can also work against you. I've read another story about the chief executive of a big corporation who fed his mind on pornography. This led to him committing an offence and he lost his job, his family, his reputation, everything.

Feed Your Imagination

You need to feed your imagination. If you'd like a new car, take one for a test drive, smell the interior, hear the engine, touch the bodywork. Get colour brochures, fabric swatches. Get emotional about it.

Emotion and imagination are the fuel that will get you closer to your dream.

Kids feed their imagination. They have posters, models, photos and things all over their bedroom walls. Rock stars, racing drivers, bikes, planes, movie stars. Surround yourself with your future.

If you don't feel confident about this I suggest that you find people who are doing what you would like to do. Listen to them, feed off their imagination and enthusiasm. The people who I regarded as my heroes back in the days when Youth Alive started out are now my peers.

Stinking Thinking

Negative thinking, like the common "It's never been done before" mentality, has hindered many a great dream: Here's a list of what negativity does

1. **Negativity cripples growth, hinders and stunts your future progress**

    How motivated do you think people will be if they're always hearing reasons why "It can't be done"? For example, your business can't grow because it's a time of recession . . . you'll never make it because you don't have the right education . . . or you can't lose weight because you've never been able to before.

2. **Negativity makes excuses rather than opportunities**

    For every opportunity you will find someone with an excuse. This is the pattern of the negative mindset. Rather, a dreamer needs to find an opportunity and take hold of it. Don't make excuses.

3. **Negativity builds doubt rather than faith**

    Negativity thrives on doubt. When we started to expand Youth Alive in order to impact the lives of young people, the voices of doubt rose up–even from so-called advisors.

I quickly learned that success is not built on the negative voice of doubt but on a foundation of faith. Faith in God. Faith in people. Faith in what you are doing.

4. Negativity reproduces itself (unfortunately) and this causes friction and division.

It is amazing how negative people can find each other in a crowd. They send out this radar beam that says "No, it's impossible, We're attempting more than we can cope with," and so on. So often in business and church life people approach a visionary or a leader and, with well-meaning constructive criticism, say such things as, "You realise what everyone is saying ..." or "I thought it was my duty to inform you that we won't reach our goal because ..."

As a dreamer don't allow yourself to be intimidated by critics. If this happens to you ask, "Who is saying . . . ?" Get the critic to define where the negatives are coming from. Many times "Everyone!" is really a handful of worriers who won't be lifting a finger to help you anyway. All they've done is send out their negativity beam and gathered together against you in unity.

Nothing deflates people more than negativity, so speak your dream and think positive!

As Bishop Fulton Sheen says, "The mind is like a clock that is constantly running down, and you need to wind it up daily with good thoughts." I like that.

5. Negativity promotes an underachiever mentality.

A positive person is one who knows they can achieve. Whether you think you can or whether you think you can't, either way you're right! A negative person is one who thinks they might achieve.

6. Negativity lacks purpose and joy.

Your mindset affects you emotionally. Negativity can cause misery and ill-health whereas positive thinking and belief can create a life of joy and satisfaction.

7. Negativity pulls down instead of building up.

People with a negative mindset always find fault. A positive mindset finds answers. The Japanese have a motto which says: "Solve the problem, don't point the blame." Simple, and very true.

8. Negativity binds the capacity to dream.

Negativity is a limitation factor. It places boundaries and limits to how far you can go, how big your business can grow, how many goals you can score in a sporting event, how much you deserve to earn in your job. On the reverse side, a positive mindset has no limits–it shoots for the stars.

9. Negativity justifies its own existence.

"I'm allowed to be what I am because of my family upbringing. I can't make it to the top because of where I live. My business went under before–I tried to make it work but I can't do it again." I'm sure you've heard many more.

10. Negativity contaminates relationships.

Negative people will always find the worst points in others. A dreamer will only see the best, and that comes out of a positive mindset.

Feel Good or Bad . . . It's Up To You

It's amazing how our thinking affects our behaviour. You choose how you behave. I read a wonderful book by Fred Smith called *You And Your Network*. Fred says we choose our moods. It's so true. You don't have to have a bad mood. You choose to. So don't. Decide to change your thinking.

Many people today are victims of all kinds of tragedies. Business or marital failure, child abuse, rejection, divorce, verbal abuse, physical abuse, racism, economic injustice and so on. Whilst I empathise with such people and spend my life trying to help them, I find the greatest tragedy is that some of them choose to remain victims. They develop a "victim mentality". They become bitter rather than better.

Consider the words of the famous motivator and sales trainer Dale Carnegie– "Feeling sorry for yourself and your present condition is not only a waste of energy but the worst habit you could possibly have."

It doesn't matter where you've been in life. What matters is where you're going. Everybody gets hurt, everybody has disappointments. Hurt is hurt and failure is failure, no matter how it's packaged. How you respond to it makes all the difference in the world.

Victory Mentality

One of the greatest motivators for living beyond victimised thinking is to get a vision for something and pursue it. If you have a dream you will develop a "victory mentality".

I've seen people living in ghettos, but the ghetto doesn't live in them. I remember working with young people in New York City and meeting the cutest little guy with the tightest curls in his hair, pants five times too big and dirty little shoes. He was carrying two huge containers of water on his shoulders and a pump action water pistol. The pistol and water tanks were bigger than he was, but that didn't stop him. He was spraying water on the walls like a madman. I thought he was playing so I said, "Hey kid, what are you doing?"

He replied as quick as a flash, "I'm cleaning up this town."

Your success in life
is not based on what has
happened in the past
but what can happen
in the future.

There was a kid who lived in the ghetto, but the ghetto didn't live in him. That's a dreamer. Some people might say his dream was just a child's dream. But I say dreams come true.

Big Thinking

None of us is an expert at everything. It's obvious that in order to achieve what you have planned for your future, you are going to have to grow, change your thinking and take on new skills. Vision will motivate you to grow and excel.

At the same time, if the dream or vision isn't important or is too small you won't have the motivation to grow. Therefore have BIG dreams.

You need the courage to dream big dreams and believe you can reach them. Here's an example I read in a book about big thinking through the eyes of a child.

A man was walking beside the sea one hot summer evening when he saw a little girl coming towards him, almost hidden behind the biggest stick of candy floss he'd ever seen. It was about two feet high and a foot wide. He laughed at the sight and when she came near he asked, "How can a little girl like you eat all of that?" Without any hesitation she replied, "Well you see, mister, I'm really much bigger on the inside than I am on the outside."

How big are you? You and I must extend our thinking. Your only limits are the ones you create. God made us big on the inside but life can make us small. Turn every situation around. It's all about your thinking.

Remember, big dreams come from big thinkers.

SUMMARY

THE HEAD
1. Don't be superficial or build a facade
2. Seek inner qualities such as honesty, integrity and truth

THE MIND
1. Think positively
2. Be solution-oriented
3. Be a creative thinker
4. Use your imagination
5. Choose your moods, attitudes and responses
6. Be a big thinker

Chapter Five

THE EYES AND EARS

Look and listen for opportunities

The visionary's eyes see where others can't. They see the future, the present as it can be, opportunities, hope in hopelessness and destiny in despair.

THE EYES

Helen Keller, the deaf and blind girl who overcame her handicaps and became such an inspiration to dreamers all over the world, was once asked, "What is worse than being blind?" Her response was "*Being able to see but having no vision.*"

I have often said that this generation is being called the first one without a potential future. Reports say that our young people feel helpless. They see governments in chaos, social values contradicting themselves, families falling apart, about one-third of marriages failing, inconsistent justice systems, businesses collapsing, people hiding behind facades of success, rising unemployment figures and nations without strong ethical leaders. The medical profession says that if heart disease, cancer, cholesterol or high blood pressure don't get you, AIDS might. If illness or AIDS don't, maybe drug or alcohol abuse might. If they don't, some power-crazy madman might press the button and we'll all go sky high. That's the cloud of despair hanging over our modern, hi-tech, advanced world. Scary, isn't it?

Dreamers dare to see differently. They see beyond the facts.

Dreamers have the ability to see things differently. Not as they are, but as they want them to be.

In her book *The Popcorn Report*, Faith Popcorn says we need to see the future so we can deal with the present. Dreamers need to see the future for their business, community, family, wife or husband, children ... and that will help them in dealing with the challenges they face now. As Dr William Menninger says: *"A fellow must know where he wants to go if he is going to get anywhere. It is so easy just to drift along."*

WAKE UP AND DREAM

Some time ago I was speaking at a church located in a rough slum part of New York City. I had just finished when I noticed a very sick-looking elderly woman in the crowd. The pastor told me she was dying of AIDS. I couldn't help but notice she had a serene angelic appearance, so I went over and introduced myself.

I mentioned that I had been told of her sickness and she explained in broken English how she contracted the disease. Her husband of 30 years had been unfaithful. He had slept with a streetwalker and then infected her. I asked how she felt and expected something like, "That rotten stinking husband of mine, I hate him". But instead she smiled and said, "Brother Pat, I know who I believe in and He is able to keep me. This disease can kill my body, but it cannot kill the One who lives inside my heart." What faith! Here was somebody living beyond the hurt and pain and unfairness of life. Here was a dreamer. A visionary. Needless to say I have told the story over and over again.

The facts were she had AIDS and was dying. The truth was it didn't have to rule her. The facts are that life might be difficult. The truth is that every obstacle is an opportunity in disguise.

Clear Focus

To be a visionary you have to have focus–to be able to aim, like an arrow, at a single target. If you allow yourself to get involved in too many things you will lose that focus. Again, I like what Dale Carnegie said about this: *"The intention, often unconscious, is to fill life so full of secondary activities or substitute activities that there will be no time in which to perform the best work of which one is capable."*

In order to maintain that tunnel vision you cannot do everything. You can only do what you are meant to do. There might be a hundred things you want to do in your business, but you need to do only the things that are necessary to fulfil your dream. Don't allow the unnecessary to take precedence over the necessary.

For example, in my work with youth there are numerous things that young people need: refuge houses, drug rehabilitation, houses for homeless, homes for the psychiatrically or psychologically affected, radio and TV stations to provide positive and uplifting entertainment, high school work, children work, training of leaders, live music concerts. The list goes on and on.

In fulfilling the Youth Alive dream we have focussed on city-wide concerts and rallies (where we refer kids back to their local church or specialised help), high school programs, community outreaches, training of leaders, training of community and business leaders.

Staying focussed on these areas will help us to achieve our mission and goals. In areas such as housing and rehabilitation there are other gifted and qualified people I can refer people to. Thus I am fulfiling my dream and the dreams of others who are in those areas.

Know who you are, and where you want to go, and keep focussed on that goal until you get there.

THE EARS

There's a biblical proverb which says *"Be quick to listen and slow to speak"*. God gave us two ears and one mouth. We should take the hint. Listen more, talk less.

Most people have it the other way around. Even as you talk to them they're thinking of what they'll say next. They're not *actively* listening. Listening has become a lost art. Everyone is ready to give advice and few are ready to hear it because they're sidetracked with giving it!

I remember a time when I was speaking to high school students and noticed a girl in the crowd who was crying. Afterwards, I sought her out and asked why she was upset. For the next twenty minutes she poured out her life to me–how she had been molested and thrown out of home. I never got a chance to say a word, which is strange for me, and at the end she said, "Thanks for listening, I just needed someone to talk to".

I gave no advice or counselling, just a listening ear. More than we realise, that's all people need.

"Nature has given to man one tongue, but two ears, that we may hear from others twice as much as we speak."
Epictetus

A friend of mine told me about how he went to a birthday party and was introduced to a very influential businessman. My friend never got a word in. At the end of the night the businessman went to a mutual friend and said that my friend John is a great communicator!

You will find it relatively easy to build friendships if you are willing to have empathy–to hear what others say and consider things through their eyes. Leaders know they can motivate people simply by listening and taking notice.

Listen to customers, to clients, to the opposition, to advice, to positives and sometimes even to negatives–but don't let them into your heart.

A while ago I was overseas with my wife, Liz, and our two daughters. On the return trip we were delayed in some obscure country for hours and it ended up being a 48 hour flight. As you can imagine, my kids got a little uncontrollable after spending all that time in such a confined area. Liz and I looked like we'd just finished ten rounds against a tag team of World Championship wrestlers!

I staggered sore and stiff over to the baggage area to get our luggage. Suddenly, a very refined lady with a mink coat and more diamonds than a jewellery store yelled, "Yoo hoo, baggage boy." I turned around under the steam of my boiling Italian blood.

Thanks to Liz's calming advice I kept an appearance of being cool. I came to realise the woman wasn't being condescending but was actually making fun of her inability to carry her own bags. While I heard "baggage boy" she was really saying "I'm old, I need help". I gave her a hand.

In that moment I was reminded to not only

listen to people's words but also to listen to the actions that accompany what is said. You can say Mary is a nice person and by a simple change of facial expression get two totally differ- ent responses from the same comment. It could be a compliment or a slur on their character.

We need to have ears that hear a person's inner cry–the cry that says "I'm not equipped to do that" or "I don't have the talent to try this". Dreamers have a genuine interest in what other people are telling them. They ask relevant and intelligent questions. They nod and use positive body language. Dreamers are good listeners.

SUMMARY

THE EYES
1. Look beyond circumstances
2. See the future, know where you're going
3. Be single-focussed, not distracted
4. You can't do everything you want, so select the most important areas

THE EARS
1. Be an active listener
2. Have empathy, genuine concern
3. Listen for the "inner cry"

Chapter Six

THE TONGUE

Speak the dream

The tongue of a dreamer always speaks words of encouragement, building others up. It uses tact and diplomacy.

Dreams live or die in our mouths. I can tell a dreamer by the words they speak. The Bible puts it more bluntly–it says life and death are in the power of the tongue. The words we use, and the thoughts and attitudes behind them, determine our future. That's a powerful statement.

Can you keep a secret? People will be open to sharing their most precious thoughts and feelings with you if they know you can. With that sharing comes a strong bond of friendship, along with opportunities for you to speak into other peoples' lives–to encourage, motivate and keep them on track towards their dream.

Impart Your Dream

One of the important things that any visionary must learn is the ability to communicate the dream, affirm the dream, repeat the dream, and impart the dream. In other words, to help others assimilate the dream.

You've read how I was motivated by that boring youth rally to take over and create something relevant and positive for young people. I told my friends what I wanted to do, I repeated it over and over again, building the picture bigger and bigger in my mind. Then I imparted the dream in the shape of Youth Alive.

Dreams live or die
in our mouths.
I can tell a dreamer
by the words they speak.

I said earlier that you need to focus on what will get you closer to your dream. This means sometimes having to include others in the process. Obviously, no-one could run Youth Alive, or any other organisation, single-handed.

To draw other people, the vision must be communicated and articulated. That way they will get a good idea of what you are doing and know if it is a part of the dreams they have for their lives, too.

Growth and productivity is only likely to occur where there is clear communication of where you are going, what you are about and what you want to achieve.

Over the years I have found that the best way to get people to see your dream is to communicate it through your words and your attitudes, and by showing them how to implement it. So you speak it, live it and show it. Put simply:

Explain your dream (words), train others to be involved in the dream (actions), allow them to participate (reproduce yourself).

See Your Dream On Paper

Write the vision out. Verbal communication is great and highly effective; however, what you say can easily be forgotten no matter how good it is. So write your dream out.

Keep it simple, exciting, to the point, and show the benefits.

You need to understand the dream, then help others do the same—its scope and its rewards. When I played football I could never understand why we had to train three days a week for an 80-minute match. It became obvious to me when our team consistently won matches that it was our coach who had the dream to win, and he communicated it to us when he told us that our game would only be as good as our preparation. He convinced us our victory would always be sweeter because of the effort we put in. How right he was.

A number of personal development books talk of writing down five or six major goals on small cards and carrying them with you in your pocket, diary, wallet or purse. Each day you read those affirmations out to yourself, telling yourself that these things are going to become reality. You write them as if the things you want to happen have already occurred, and you include how you are feeling as a result.

An example could be: "I have doubled my sales record for the month and sold $20,000 worth of stock. I have achieved the $500 bonus and bought the grey microweave double-breasted suit I really wanted and it looks fantastic on me. My manager has more respect for me and I feel very confident about my sales skills."

Repeat Your Dream

Repeat your vision over and over again. I tell the young people I am involved with that we are going to fill such and such an auditorium, and I repeat the dream until they see it for themselves. They see it as much as I can, or at least as much as is possible.

Their attitude then becomes "It's our dream, not just his dream." At Youth Alive each member of the team owns the vision. It is not just Pat's dream.

Affirmation is an important element in dreaming. It means restating your plans for the future over and over so that they are ingrained into your mind. It can be done in numerous ways.

One important but neglected way of affirming your dream is by not doing other things. Let's face it, there are a lot of great ideas but not all of them are going to help you achieve what you want for your life. If that's the case, don't get involved. Don't race off with every new idea presented to you. Weigh it up against your plan for the future, and if it isn't relevant, forget it.

Speak The Dream Into Existence

If people don't know your obsession or dream, you probably don't have one. I remember when Youth Alive started off I kept saying that one day we would fill the largest venue in our city–the Entertainment Centre. At that stage it seemed highly unlikely, but as our movement kept getting larger and filled bigger and bigger venues, it became clear we were on the way to fulfilling the dream.

As far as we were concerned there was no turning back, no alternative. We had a purpose–to help people find more to life than activities which waste their potential–and we owned that vision. We thought about it and talked about it every day.

When you decide on something don't be casual about it. Own it. Allow it to become a big part of you.

SUMMARY

THE TONGUE
1. Speak encouragement, positively
2. Choose words wisely
3. Be trustworthy; keep confidences
4. Communicate your dream
5. Affirm your dream
6. Repeat your dream
7. Impart your dream
8. Write your dream down
9. Repeat your dream over and over out loud (use cards)
10. Own your dream
11. Talk about your dream daily

Chapter Seven

THE BACKBONE

Plan to succeed

The backbone supports the body. It is the structure of the body and all dream-building requires structure. It's more than thinking fuzzy thoughts. If you don't have a plan, you're planning to go nowhere.

Dreams without strategies are simply wishful thinking.

No dream is without a strategy. If you want to build a house you need architectural plans, building materials, foundations, and so on. Many people run their businesses, churches or organisations with the principle.

READY . . .FIRE! . . . AIM. They're shooting at a hundred things hoping to hit one.

Dr Fitzhugh Dodson is quoted as saying: "Without goals and plans to reach them you are like a ship that has set sail with no destination".

Dreams need to be turned into goals—measurable goals, with deadlines—so that you can analyse your progress. As the saying goes.

If you aim for nothing, you'll probably hit it.

First of all you need to work out how long you plan to take to reach your dream, to see it become reality. Let's say it's five years. Divide your goals into years, then into months, weeks, and days. Decide what has to be done today, tomorrow, and this week to get you on track to this month's goal, which will lead on to next month's goal, and so on.

Get Smart

Goals need to be S.M.A.R.T.
That is:
- **Specific**
- **Measurable**
- **Action-oriented**
- **Realistic**
- **Timetabled**

Review your plan daily. Keep it in a daily planner at the front of your diary for quick reference. Develop a habit of going over your goals morning and night. Take time to check how well you're progressing, and, if you find yourself slipping in a certain area, adjust the goal–don't criticise or condemn yourself.

The strategy is as important as the dream. Imagine getting on a plane and the pilot saying after take-off, "We don't have a flight plan but we're making good progress." Without a strategy you can't set a course, you can't pace yourself, you can't measure your progress, and others can't follow you.

This is why dreamers need strategists and those gifted in areas of administration to implement their dreams. Generally speaking, visionaries are not organisers or strategists. And strategists and organisers tend not to be risk-taking dreamers. The two don't disqualify each other, they complement each other.

Have Plan "B"

Sometimes plans go wrong. If you prepare for something to go wrong you'll be mentally ready and the obstacle won't throw you.

Award-winning motivational author and speaker Charlie "Tremendous" Jones says plans need to be flexible so when something goes wrong you can reshape the plan. He says: *"Plan on your plan going wrong so that you're ready with an alternative plan because that's my plan!"*

Be careful–it is possible to plan yourself out of creativity and vision. You can over-plan. Plans are not meant to box you in. They're there to launch you into your destiny, not to stifle you. And they shouldn't make you miserable.

Don't Just Write It . . . DO IT!!!

When you take the time to plan your future, avoid the mistake of ignoring the plan. Make sure you work it. If you run into trouble, set smaller bite-size goals which lead up to the end-goal. And offer yourself rewards along the way.

If a plan is working, stick to it. Don't deviate from it or re-invent the wheel. Yes, use your own creativity, but if something ain't broken, don't try to fix it!

Daily Successes

You are not a successful person only when you achieve your dream. Each step in your plan gives you the opportunity for achievement.

When I drastically changed the youth rallies years ago to include rock music and punchy, relevant speakers, I felt successful. Regardless of how many kids came to see us, I had caused change. When I was forced to seek bigger and bigger venues, I felt successful.

When I speak to hundreds and hundreds of people and they tell me how Youth Alive is helping them get new positive direction in life, I feel successful. When I see top name performers at our rallies, I feel successful. When we move to a huge football stadium one day I will feel successful.

But that's only in one area of my life.

As my relationship with my wife and daughters has grown and grown, I have felt success. As my ability to travel the world and impart hope and motivation to more and more people to change their lives has increased, I have experienced success. As I have moved from a tiny house to a newer, more comfortable one, I have felt success. As I have gone from a run down car that rattled and shook to a modern vehicle that's as quiet as a mouse, I have felt success. As I have grabbed opportunities to speak to large groups of business people and had a part to play in their lives taking a positive turn, I have felt successful. And as I have developed my time management skills more and more to give my life a better balance, I have felt successful.

Reaching your dream is a constant improvement process right across the board: personal life, finances, lifestyle, business life, social life, relationships, and so on.

I mentioned my wife and daughters just now, and I want to stress that they are very much part of my dream. My family means everything to me. Including them in my dream is part of having a solid backbone.

The backbone helps the body stay balanced, and dream-building is all about balance. Truly successful dreamers keep their lives in equilibrium. The best dreams cover every important aspect of life and neglect none.

In both your dream and your plan to reach that dream, you need to consider all parts of your life–not just your vision for business success, sporting victory or helping others. Be honest with yourself. If it takes a hundred hours a week to pursue a financial goal, will your family or health suffer?

---

*Success is only success
if it's success
in all areas of life.*

I love to look at how different dreamers endured the odds and reached their goals. Sadly, some of these people have sacrificed everything in order to reach them. I'm a firm believer in living a balanced life. Your family is more important than your business. If you put your business first you might just lose both.

A song that came out recently was an old Harry Chapin hit that was re-released. Called *"Cat's in the Cradle,"* it speaks about a Dad who has a boy. He's very busy so they don't spend much time together. The boy grows up, the father says how proud he is of him and how he would now like them to spend time together. But the son says he'd really like to go out with his friends. At the end of the song, the teenager is a father himself, and the father is an old man with lots of time on his hands. But the son is too busy with work. The boy turned out just like him.

What we do in our family will be reproduced for generations to come. If you neglect your kids, they will neglect theirs. Too many people sacrifice their families for their careers. Though you might score an A-plus in business, if it's accompanied by a D-minus in family life you won't feel like a success.

Success is only success if it's success in all areas of life.

Value your wife or husband and kids. When you go home, brighten up. Don't go off the handle and take out all your disillusionment and frustration on them. If you verbally stab your family you will produce bleeding hearts.

Take time out and learn to make and keep appointments with your family. I travel extensively, and one thing I have learned to do (which has not been easy for me) is to switch off work and switch on to my family.

I believe that every person needs to have as a major part of their dream the desire to have a stable, loving, sharing and caring family.

I know there are some sad examples out there–believe me, I talk to them every week–but I have also seen cases where people were able to overcome seemingly impossible odds to restore their homes because they clung to a belief that it could happen.

The Four T's

This matter of including your family in your dream is so important that I want to share with you what I tell people in my parent-teen seminars. It's called The Four T's.

1. Time

Quality time is good time and a lot of time. Some people excuse themselves by saying, "We have quality time and watch the TV". That's not quality time, it's a waste of time. Quality time is an investment in others.

2. Talk

One of the greatest complaints is that families don't communicate any more. I read once where the average family in America only talks a few minutes each week. Yeah, each week!

As mentioned in chapter six, sometimes talking is listening. Liz often likes to find some quieter-than-normal time during the week and talk to me for ages; then she commends me on being such a great communicator. She wants a listening ear.

Don't talk about negatives. Ask questions, and get beyond the "usual" questions like "How was your day?" You know the standard answer: "Good."

How familiar does this sound?

Child says to parent: "Can I?"

Parent: "No."

Child: "Can I buy?"

Parent: "No."

Child: "Can I have?"

Parent: "No."

Parents come from parent planet and they only learn one word: No. Kids come from teenager planet and they only know one word: Why? And the standard reply to that is: "Cause I said so."

Teenager: "That's no reason."

Parent: "One more word out of you and you'll get it!"

Teenager: "Uh?"

Parent: "Do you want a belting?" (As if the parent somehow expects the child to jump up and say "Yes, please.")

There has to be more to communication than "No" and "Why?" and "Cause I said so." Ask your partner and kids questions that require clever answers. Find out how they think. Ask them for their dreams. Talking is one of the most fun things you can do.

3. Touch

There is nothing more wonderful than touching your partner and children, helping them feel appreciated and loved. A hug, a pat on the back or a kiss lets them know they are appreciated, esteemed and respected.

One of the saddest scenes I've ever seen was at an airport. A family stood not far away from me and it was obvious the little boy's Dad had been away for a while. His adoring son waited excitedly. Suddenly, the father came through the arrival gate. The little boy's eyes lit up and, with a big smile on his face, he ran over to hug him. The father just stuck his hand out and shook his son's hand.

This is supposedly a manly gesture. But that little boy needed to be hugged, kissed and loved. I often wonder how that episode will affect his life in the future.

4. Tenderness

One of the saddest things about men in the

1990s is that they expect to be macho men as though it's not right to have feelings or be tender. That isn't a man. That's a wall.

A real man can express feelings. It's okay to cry, to feel and express tenderness. Tenderness is important in a home.

Your family will reflect the kind of person you are, so make sure it's a true mirror and a true reflection of your character. Guys–it's OK to cry.

In addition to these Four T's, there are a few other tips about family life that I believe are simple but powerful.

Don't say or do anything you don't want your family to do. Watch your mouth. Words are remembered long after they are spoken. Avoid put-downs or generalisations that hurt.

Keep short accounts with each other. Don't let arguments last longer than they have to. There's a Bible verse that says, *"Don't let the sun go down on your anger."* In other words, deal with situations straight away before they get out of control. Even if you are right, make the first step to reconciliation. Relationships are worth more than who wins the arguments.

It's A Family Affair

If you have family, share your dreams with your partner and kids. Make them a part of it.

Don't hold it to yourself saying "You wouldn't understand". You'd be surprised what they understand. The simplest answers can often come out of the simplest hearts.

Make sure your family is part of your backbone.

Passing The Buck

Lack of accountability–lack of backbone–is a big hindrance to achieving your vision. Everyone answers to somebody, at work, at home, on the sporting field.

If you are in a position of leadership, it is vital that you be held accountable for your actions. I've heard people say, "I'm accountable to nobody." That's a wonderful plan for failure.

This disease has got other symptoms such as the one more commonly known to us as *passing-the-buck-itis.* Common features of this condition include the following:

- Blaming others for your mistakes (blame-itis).
- Taking no responsibility for your own actions.
- Taking no responsibility for the actions of those under your leadership.
- Using excuses such as "I'm a visionary, not an organiser" or "It wasn't my job anyway".

- Never attempting things "outside the box" which could be stretching.
- Generally lacking backbone and being a wimp–boring, unexciting, moody, depressed, discouraged and insular.

We live in a world where *passing-the-buck-itis* is at epidemic proportions. No-one wants to take responsibility any more. But real dreamers don't distance themselves from accountability. You're the dreamer, the vision-ary, the leader ... and the buck stops with you.

Here are the qualities of true dreamers who are prepared to be accountable:

- They accept responsibility–*"the buck stops here"*.
- They set direction, speak direction, show direction and lead by example.
- They give responsibility to others with clar-ity and vision. They delegate authority.
- They admit their mistakes and learn from errors, making every effort not to repeat them.
- They take risks and dare to do things dif-ferently. They're open to change and adjustment along the way.
- They're excited, enthusiastic, not given to extreme mood swings. They decide how they will act and react.
- They only speak positively.

Leaders grow on responsibility, and, by delegating it, they encourage others to become responsible also. If your organisation is not progressing, if your business isn't making a profit, then take a look at yourself. This advice may seem harsh, cold and blunt, but dreamers and leaders are people who take on responsibility, are accountable for their actions, and run with them.

---

*Staying accountable
helps us focus.
It keeps us honest.
It keeps us on track.*

We live in a Western culture that wants to run from responsibilities. Dad runs from home with his young secretary and leaves a trail of broken-hearted kids and a devastated wife. I believe the reason we have runaway kids is because we have runaway parents. We have irresponsible kids because we have irresponsible leaders who don't want to teach, train and delegate duties. If leaders, governments, corporate executives and pastors don't take upon themselves the privilege of responsibility, those under them will not run with any vision or dream. They will live in defeat.

I am accountable to a great team of men and women who meet regularly. They ask about my finances, my family, my commitment. It's important. People who run from accountability crash straight into disaster. If you have people around you who have your dream and vision as their priority, they will give you good advice.

Staying accountable helps us focus. It keeps us honest. It keeps us on track.

SUMMARY

THE BACKBONE
1. Plan for your dream
2. Turn your dream into goals–years, months, weeks, days
3. Make your goals S.M.A.R.T.
4. Use a day planner
5. Pace yourself
6. Let your plans be flexible
7. Don't over-plan
8. Seek balance in all areas of life
9. Value family and relationships
10. Be accountable

Chapter Eight

THE HANDS

Dreaming is hard work

D reamers are hard workers. They have "doing" hands that do what needs to be done. They also reach out to others, embrace others' skills to compensate for their own weaknesses, and are giving and generous.

On the subject of hard workers, have a read of Proverbs chapter six verses 6–11 in the Bible. This illustration looks at the busy ant who never stops; he's always gathering food or repairing his home. Therefore during winter he has enough to eat, and he always has a place to live. It's simple but worth noting.

There's really no excuse for avoiding hard work. All worthwhile dreams require as much perspiration as they do inspiration.

The Place To Begin

Hands write, and, as I mentioned earlier, it's important to begin by writing your dream down on paper. I've read that less than 5% of the population actually write down their goals and vision.

An example I read was of a graduating class from America's prestigious Harvard University. A research team randomly asked one hundred students what they wanted to be doing in ten years' time. Most of the answers included running big companies, being rich and famous, or affecting the world in some way for the better.

Out of those 100 people, only 10 had bothered to write down their goals, clearly describing what they were after. Ten years later the same researchers tracked down the same group of graduates and found that the 10 who had written down their goals owned 96% of the combined wealth of the 100 people. 96%! Powerful.

I spend a lot of time thinking about what I want to achieve. I share my thoughts with my closest friends and write down simple statements which explain to me the complete picture. You don't have to be a professional writer or come up with 10 volumes of notes. A multitude of words creates confusion. Keep it basic.

Link In With Others

Dreamers use their hands to link up with other dreamers, and to pull along (encourage and motivate) the people they are with.

As I also noted earlier, you need to include other people in your plans, as I have done with the constantly expanding Youth Alive. In this case, it's important to impart your dream to faithful people, not necessarily the most able ones. You can find an able person more easily than a loyal person.

Faithful people will have your interests and your dream at heart, with no personal hidden agendas. It might be that a loyal person is also an able person. If that's the case, you're doing well.

Impart your dream to faithful and loyal people. You will change their lives, and they will help you change yours.

I would rather have a faithful person than an able person. It's easier to make a faithful person able than to change the heart of a very capable but disloyal person. The Bible mentions an interesting principle, which might be paraphrased as follows: *"He who is faithful in what is least is faithful in much, and he who is unjust in what is least is unjust in what is much. And if you have been faithful in what is another man's, he will give you your own."*

Don't Point The Finger

Hands have fingers, but dreamers don't point the finger–or judge others. There's a principle in the Bible that sums it up: treat other people as nicely as you'd like them to treat you. You can't say it any simpler than that. Judging is negative and often wrong.

I heard a story about a businessman travelling in a plane. He was sitting near a guy with tattoos, long hair, earrings, a ring through his nose and scruffy clothes. He got up the courage to talk to this guy and found out he was a university graduate who was quite intelligent, involved in the arts and had a great personality. Don't judge a book by its cover.

Helping Others Achieve Their Dreams

Part of my goal and reason for being a leader is to help others in Youth Alive to be inspired to fulfil their dreams, not to be threatened by their abilities and giftings but to nurture them.

We have creative people, administrative people and technical people. Some of them love numbers, others can't count to save themselves. Some people wire up sound and lighting systems, others can type quickly. Together they all contribute to the dream.

In being faithful to other people's visions and dreams I've found I've been able to fulfil my own. There are many wonderful illustrations of this principle.

There is a Bible story told of a young Israelite warrior called David. At one stage he was fleeing the evil and jealous king of Israel–the man he would replace. While he hid from search parties in caves in the desert, a group of men came to him. They were disgruntled, in debt and in distress. Social outcasts.

Outwardly these guys had nothing to offer the great soldier, yet he became their leader. Later on we find that these same men became skilled warriors. They went from being criminals to national heroes. At one stage, when David desired to drink water from a certain well deep in enemy territory, some of these soldiers sneaked out and took water for him to drink.

What was it about these guys? How did they change so dramatically? They were united in vision with David. The test wasn't their abilities but their hearts. No hidden agendas, no sedition, just hearts that were completely loyal. And David recognised their value in his life.

I cannot say it enough. If you want to be a dreamer, a person who will make a difference in your life and others', you must be willing to link hands with people around you. See their value to you. As John Donne said–*"No man is an island"*.

Changing Through Friendships

Dreamers extend a hand of friendship, support and love. They don't walk around with their hands in their pockets. One of the world's top motivational speakers, Zig Ziglar, puts it this way: "You can get everything in life you want if you help enough other people get what they want." And Harvey Firestone of tyre fame said: "You get the best out of others when you give the best of yourself."

Self-help books, tapes and videos I have been exposed to major on getting people to change their behaviour. Whilst I find these tools totally necessary, I believe the best way to motivate people to change is through friendship.

When two people are in love they do things that please each other. They want to be better–to dress better, look better, behave better, smell better! If you're inspired in business by friendship, you'll have the same response. You'll want to be a better person. And your actions will rub off on others.

I have a friend who is a sharp dresser and

has the ability to wear unbelievable ties–whereas I always had the art of choosing the most boring ones. However, today I am a tie connoisseur and look almost as sharp as he does! It's a little thing but it's an example of how we all rub off on each other.

How To Build Relationships

I am constantly dealing with relationships when I go to high schools, Youth Alive rallies and business seminars. I see the victims of broken relationships which confirm over and over again to me the importance of investing in friendships. I produced a book a while ago about friendship because it means so much to me, and I touched on the following areas. I believe they relate to the subject of dreaming.

1. People or Profit

People are more important than profit. It's a pity many business leaders don't realise that. Money doesn't feel, people do. Don't get me wrong–profit is good. But it must not come at the expense of people.

Until recent times a man's word was his bond. He didn't need contracts in triplicate with pages of fine print. Today you can have a person's word and a contract, but it isn't their bond because what is important to them is the profit margin. We see contracts being broken everyday in marriage, sport and the business world because of selfish motives. In many cases, those involved are a lot worse off for breaking their agreements.

I believe an environment where a team of loyal, dedicated business people work together in unison is far more effective than an environment controlled by the almighty dollar where there is no job security or trust.

2. Build Bridges Not Walls

As you go through the day-to-day motions of pursuing your dream, stay real, approachable and open. There can be a tendency for dream-builders to become aloof and distant because they are on a mission. They don't want to be distracted, slowed down or criticised by those who can't understand what they're up to.

Friendships can build you bridges to where you want to go and open up windows of opportunity.

3. Here, There and Everywhere

To be imparted, your dream must be omnipresent. In other words, it must be in everything that you do. Always with you. Then others will catch it.

Here's an example. A few years ago a young lady came to our office with a desire to work with young people. She decided to come on staff without pay. Anybody who does that has got to be committed–or stupid!. Or another option–extremely committed. Lyn immersed herself in the all-pervasive dream of Youth Alive. She was not skilled but was willing to learn. Today she basically runs our functions. She knows how I think, what I like and don't like. In fact, she knows me better than I know me.

One day a man said, "You'd better enjoy this while it lasts, because one day Youth Alive won't exist." You should have seen the look on Lyn's face. She said, "There is no reason on God's earth why His dream has to end. The only ones who could kill it are us."

Lyn has become one of my most reliable, trustworthy people, and she in turn is now training others. A faithful person who became able is now imparting to others the Youth Alive vision.

That's the kind of person who will help you–a person who will get their hands dirty with you in the hard work of bringing about your dream.

SUMMARY

THE HANDS:
1. Embrace other people
2. Be a hard worker
3. Link in with other dreamers
4. Don't point the finger (judge others)
5. Write your vision
6. Keep it simple
7. Find faithful people to work with
8. Be approachable

Chapter Nine

THE HEART

Care your way to success

C haracter, integrity, commitment, endurance, faith–the heart of a dreamer.

The heart of a dreamer is filled not only with dreams but with a love for people, valuing people more than things. It is compassionate, not ruthless. A dreamer's heart is tender, strong, teachable, merciful, full of courage and responsible. It doesn't hold grudges and it's arteries remain uncluttered by anger, resentment or bitterness.

A college student once asked me, with a self-righteous I-know-it-all attitude, why I do what I do. I led the young man outside to a busy road with a lot of traffic. It was raining cats and dogs. I said if he would promise to do something for me, I would tell him why. To my surprise, he took the challenge.

I asked the student to stand in the rain without an umbrella and count the cars for two hours. I left him there for that time then returned to find his hair matted down, his nice clothes dripping all over the floor, and in his hand a soggy piece of paper with pen marks on it.

I asked him how many cars he'd seen. The answer was in the hundreds. I asked how many people had been in the cars. He gave me an estimate, in the thousands. I asked one final question: "How many people in those cars desperately need their lives put back together? How many have made wrong decisions and need help with their families, businesses, relationships, finances?"

He looked at me in amazement and said, "Probably all of them."

"That's why I do what I do," I replied. "They need help."

Me, myself and you

There is more to life than me-ism, living for personal gratification. Life is all about contributing to other people.

I'll never forget the time one of my volunteer helpers wrote a beautiful letter to me after a Youth Alive rally. I had just flown in from overseas and was really tired. I got up on stage and in my usual manner jumped and shouted around with the band. It was a good crowd, about 10,000 kids. At the end of the night I went and talked to the workers at the different stands, the stage management team and the technical crew and thanked them for a good job well done. In his letter this helper said it was the nicest thing he'd seen and since then he has become one of our most loyal workers. But it was this first little letter that made me feel cared for, yet all I had done was show concern and care for others.

Healing Of The Heart

Many of us, however, can't show that kind of concern and care. We have broken hearts that cause us a lot of pain and actually hinder us including the welfare of others in our dreams. Our hearts need healing.

One of the worst obstacles to caring is the hurt we receive at the hands of other people and the bitterness we allow to grow from that hurt.

I read a story once about a young person who stabbed an elderly man to death in Central Park. It was a brutal killing; the man was stabbed many times. The police were puzzled. What was the motive? They asked the boy why he did it.

"Did you know him?"

"No."

"Did he talk to you?"

"No."

"Have you ever met him before?"

"No."

"Did he hurt you?"

"No."

"Did he hurt your parents?"

"No."

Hours later the 16-year-old broke down and cried and began to tell all. The story was that his brother was a great sportsman, good looking, and his father would brag about him. He would compare brothers and ask why his younger son couldn't be like the older one. The boy's younger sister won all the beauty contests and got great grades at school. The 16-year-old was told he was an accident and would never amount to anything. So, he decided to do the most hideous thing he could to become famous.

Hurt can very easily turn into bitterness. From a seed it can grow into a deeply-rooted weed.

Bitterness Is A Curse

The seeds of bitterness produce a lifetime of hurt, insecurity, suspicion and paranoia. Have you ever walked into a room with people laughing and thought "Why are they laughing at me? What are they saying about me?" This arises from an insecurity. It's very likely the other people are talking about something completely different.

One of the saddest cases of bitterness I have ever met was a young prostitute on the Gold Coast. We had staged a wonderful rally and this girl responded to my invitation to be prayed for, to receive healing from past hurts. She began to share her story of stepping into prostitution. Liz and I invited her to come to the beach with us the next day.

The following afternoon we waited on the sand. We had to be there at one o'clock. One o'clock ticked by. One-thirty. Quarter to two. Eventually at two o'clock she turned up.

"Why were you late?" I asked.

"I talked to God and said if this guy is for real you make him wait and that will be a sign," she replied. I was so glad we had stayed.

We sat down and relaxed in the warm Queensland sun. Gradually the rest of the girl's story came out. Her father had raped her when she was young. I noticed skin grafts on her legs–he had abused her physically too. She became a prostitute to get back at men. She said that by getting married men to commit an act of adultery she had power over them. Fortunately her story has a beautiful ending. This young woman wanted to be free from her bitterness and the ruin it was making of her life. She never returned to that lifestyle and started to be transformed into a happy, well-balanced human being.

But her experience illustrates how ugly the fruits of bitterness can be.

Four Simple Steps To Overcoming Bitterness

When discussing the subject of bitterness and hurts with young people I sometimes outline four principles for overcoming them:

1. **Make a list of the people who have wronged or hurt you.**

2. **Write down what you have done to hurt others.**

3. **Throw the list in the bin. Even better, burn it.**

4. **Forgive the offenders.**

Seriously, you have to be willing to forgive. That doesn't mean life becomes instantly happy and blissful, but it does release any emotional bondage you're under. Have you ever noticed how unforgiveness and bitterness put a knot in your stomach?

---

*Dump negatives. Get rid of them.
Open up that file in your head
called Dirty Rotten Filthy Things
People Have Done To Me
and throw it away ... for good!!!
No peeking at it later on.*

If there's a motto for my life it's "Keep sweet". No matter what people say about you–keep sweet. If people criticise your dream–keep sweet. If they abuse your generosity–keep sweet. If others succeed and prosper and you feel like you are missing out–keep sweet. When things don't go as planned–keep sweet.

Bitterness is a curse, and keeping it in your heart will rob you of your dreams. Get rid of it now.

Accept yourself.

Another major obstacle to caring for others is not caring for yourself. Jesus Christ said: *"Love your neighbour as you love yourself."* It's difficult to show concern for others if you won't accept yourself.

A dreamer needs a self-accepting heart.

The late Charles Spurgeon said: *"Beware of no man more than yourself; we carry our worst enemies within us."* Have you ever noticed when you look in the mirror you instantly see what is wrong, rather than your good points?

In the movie *Pretty Woman* there is a scene where Richard Gere, the successful business-man, tells Julia Roberts, the prostitute, what a great person she is (Well, what else would you say to Julia Roberts!) She says, in effect: It's hard to believe you're good at anything when all you've been told all your life is how bad you are.

We accept other people with their faults and weaknesses, but so often we won't accept ourselves. Our hair isn't right, we're too short, too tall, not tanned, not talented and so on.

But consider this: when you were con-ceived there were hundreds of millions of potential people all racing to be the first to the egg. And guess what? You won! If you've never achieved anything else of greatness in your life so far, that's certainly something to pat your-self on the back about.

You are you and there's no-one else like you. No other person (not even if you are a twin or triplet) has the same hair, eyes, skin, thoughts, likes and dislikes, dreams. Art col-lectors are willing to pay millions for one beautiful painting because . . . there is only one. You are worth more than a painting.

Enjoy other people's success

One of the consequences of accepting your own uniqueness is accepting that others are special too.

A secure dreamer has a heart that rejoices at others people's victories and is not glad when they face difficult times.

Many of my friends are successful pastors and conference speakers. I can honestly say that when they succeed in a particular area, or experience prosperity, I am happy for them.

I am not threatened by their gains because I have learned to be happy and content with my destiny in life. They challenge and motivate me to new heights, and I do the same to them. God has unique and exciting life plans for all of us.

Make your friend's success a motivator in your life rather than something that pulls you back. Be happy about it and be glad to be associated with them–after all, it makes you look good too!

Freedom from bitterness and self-acceptance are just two qualities of the real dreamer's heart. I want to describe a few more.

Integrity

One of the greatest quotes of all time is: *"To thine own self be true. Keep a clear and pure conscience. Be honest with people and yourself."*

One night I was with friends at a pizza restaurant. It was very busy–the queue went back to the door, the waitresses were racing around taking orders, the kitchen looked like mayhem. The girl who was the shift manager took the phone off the hook so as to give the impression to potential customers that it was engaged. Obviously she had no financial interest in the profitability of the place. All she had to do was put someone in charge and explain there was a wait. I will never be ordering pizzas from there again.

*You can't have a
little bit of integrity.
You either have it,
or you don't!*

You might ask why? Because she lacked integrity. Her boss employed her to make money and to work hard, not to lose money and customers. I can assure you, if she had been the owner she would have managed it a lot better.

Integrity is something that comes from within. In the movie *City Slickers*, Billy Crystal plays a young upwardly-mobile yet struggling-with-mid-life-crisis character. In one scene, one of the three "City Slickers" says to Billy, "Wouldn't you like to get some of that?" –referring to an attractive woman riding on the cattle trail with them.

Billy replies, "No". This starts an argument.

"But what if no-one knew. Just imagine the most beautiful woman in the world came down from space and wanted to make passionate love with you, then fly away, and no-one would know. Wouldn't you do it?"

"No, I wouldn't."

The upset friend challenges him, "But no-one would know."

Billy's response is so powerful, "Yes, but I'd know."

That's the key. Your reputation is what people think you are; your integrity is what you know you are. It's a heart matter.

Honesty Is The Best Policy

If integrity is what you are and your repu-tation is what other people think you are, your credibility is what other people *know* you are.

Author Fred Smith says: *"It is better to be esteemed and respected than applauded."*

I was speaking at a business conference on selling and I stated that one of the greatest keys to selling is honesty. Not all salespeople will agree with me here. If you listen to how some sales "greats" teach their craft, they're nothing more than con artists.

Integrity is being real and speaking truth.

If you have a product–like shampoo for example–that everybody needs, don't come up with some weird sales pitch like, "This shampoo not only cleans hair, it also causes internal massaging of the brain, leading to stimulation of thought patterns, which in turn create highly intelligent beings." Just say how good it is and why it is so good. And tell the truth: everyone wants clean hair. Don't manipulate by making promises you can't live up to.

Keep your integrity in the office. If you are in and don't want to take calls, don't get someone to say you're out. That's lying, and it undermines your integrity. Say you're busy on another project, take a message and call back properly. If staff and peers perceive you as a liar, that perception will distort the rest of their opinions about you.

Integrity and honesty are all too rare in our society today. One of the greatest compliments I've ever received came from a teenager at one of our rallies. He said, "You're the realest person I've ever met."

It doesn't get much better than that!

Protect Your Character At All Costs

I often cringe at some of the self-help books I read and messages I hear from motivational authors and speakers who tend to treat people as objects to be manipulated. I fear for the businessmen, executives, clergymen or community leaders who, on their way to climbing the ladder of success, step all over others and have no values to build their life upon. What you are will be reflected in what you do. If you have no character or integrity, it will show through.

People quickly forget your talents and abilities, but they never forget your character. No compromise, honesty, integrity: these are seldom used words in today's society. It's sad but it seems that all that is important to some people is the profit margin, not the quality of their work or the character of people in their organisation.

If you're a dreamer, here's a big tip: keep high standards.

People's true opinion of you is what they say about you when you aren't around. If you're dishonest and lie to clients and associates, then that's how they'll see you. Keep strong values. Have a business based on good ethics. Share these ethics with your staff.

Another thing: be seen to be a generous person with needy organisations.

Although we in Youth Alive have often needed help, we have a policy to give to those in need also. I believe that by giving you can expect to receive–it's a principle of sowing and reaping. *"Give and it will be given back to you"*, says the Bible.

Commitment

Commitment is another quality of a dreamer's heart. It's a funny word, a word people don't like. But there's never been a time when it's needed more than now. It seems to be a lost value in our modern era.

This generation needs to be committed to success, to personal fulfilment and to having commitment as its foundation.

There has to come a point in our life where something means everything to us. In *City Slickers*, the old cowboy offers advice to the character played by Billy Crystal: "One thing matters in life."

"What is it?", asks Billy.

"That's what you have to find out."

One of the opposites of commitment is quitting. The quitting attitude: what a common obstacle!

I'm convinced that many people give up too easily. They can be so close to breakthrough yet they stop short. How ridiculous! You're not meant to stop. Ever.

Dreamers have to be committed people–to themselves, their world, their neighbours, their vision.

Difficult times–financial, managerial, structural, family, home–should be a learning process. Not an excuse to quit.

If Henry Ford had quit we might never have had a motor car for the common man. If Edison had quit we might still be using gas lamps rather than electric light bulbs. Or having to write letters rather than use the phone. A never-say-quit attitude helps people see positive in everything.

"If you want to be successful, know what

you are doing, love what you are doing, and believe in what you are doing," says Will Rogers. And the Chinese philosopher Confucius said: *"Our greatest glory is not in never failing but in rising every time we fall."*

Faith

There are all sorts of ways of fostering a never-say-quit attitude, but the most important is faith.

Faith, as the Bible puts it, is the substance of things HOPED for, the evidence of things NOT SEEN. Dreams inspire faith and faith creates the ability to dream.

Faith is an incredible thing. To put it simply, it is *believing.*

We live in a world that believes a little in everything and not much in a lot. Consequently people go nowhere fast. Faith and dreams point you in a definite direction.

Belief is the fuel that keeps you moving all the way to the finish line–belief in your abilities, your chances of success, your dream. Take belief away and you'll find it difficult to keep going.

You need to believe in yourself, believe in others, believe in your dream and believe in your strategy to reach that dream. You can do it. Believe it!

Get Excited!

A consequence of not having a dream is that you don't enjoy what you're doing. It's important that what you do excites you.

I'm very proud of Youth Alive. I defend it. Once a person came to a concert and he didn't like the music so he decided to tell me. I said, "My friend, it's called Youth Alive not *Barely Alive!*"

Love what you do
and be proud of it.
Be proud of who you are
and what you represent.

I love what I do: speaking to people. I love not only what I do but why I do it. Helping people find their God-given potential in life gives me a wonderful sense of achievement. I'd speak at the drop of a hat (even if I had to drop the hat!). I'm excited by my dream. I want to make Youth Alive the youth culture of my nation and beyond. When we're finished with Earth we'll go to Mars!

I've heard some people say if I they had my job travelling around, talking to people, inspiring them, writing books and so on they'd enjoy it too. But all work involves monotony, administration, concern, challenges, preparation, weariness, problems.

I once complained to my wife, "I don't need the pressures of finances, or of worrying if the crowds come to our events, or of people misinterpreting what I say or how I do things." Liz said, "Yes you do." And the crazy thing about it is, she's right.

Where there's a dream or vision, the love for the work causes the less glamorous aspects to fade away into insignificance.

Patience And Kindness

I cringe when I think of how some bosses treat their staff. They consider them as slaves or meat in the marketplace. Common courtesies such as patience, kindness and encouragement are necessary to making and furthering friendships.

Not so long ago a big American employment firm conducted a survey of the general managers of the top one hundred corporations in New York. They wanted to find out what character traits are thought to be the most valuable for people aspiring to become top executives. Their advice was:
- Honesty and fairness
- Never compromise on matters of principle

or standards of excellence, even on minor issues

- Be persistent, never give up
- Have a vision of where you are going, communicate it often
- Know what you stand for
- Don't be afraid to take on tough problems, despite the risks involved
- Spend less time managing and more time leading (by example)
- Bring out the best in others
- Hire the best people you can find, then delegate them authority and responsibility
- Have confidence in yourself and those around you
- Accept blame for failures and credit others with success
- Have integrity and courage

These qualities don't come out of weakness, but strength. Patience comes out of character. Courtesy and kindness isn't a result of having no backbone; it comes from a position of security.

If you're in a position of authority, be patient, kind and courteous with your staff. I've often heard in management training that bosses aren't to be buddies with their staff. There is a difference between familiarity and friendship. My employees and I enjoy a wonderful friendship, but they are not familiar. I am a man under the authority of those I respect and admire. We are friends but not familiar. I help them with their dreams, and they help me to fulfil my dream with Youth Alive.

Jesus Christ said love your neighbour as you love yourself. Well, it's difficult to show concern for others if you won't accept yourself first, isn't it?

Sharing

In your body you have many different organs but they all work together. If your top half wants to go shopping and the bottom wants to go fishing, you have two options: cut yourself in half or decide where to go. The body works together to achieve whatever task it will.

I have a friend who is one of the most consistent songwriters I have ever known. His songs have touched the hearts of thousands. Can you imagine if this dreamer wrote the songs and only sang them to himself? What a waste! His personal dream of songwriting is shared by many people and we all share in his dream.

A beautiful expression of working together happened a few years ago at the special Olympics for handicapped athletes. They lined up for the start, the gun went off and all these kids with different disabilities started staggering down the track. They were a sight to see.

Suddenly, one of them stumbled and fell. The other runners stopped, went back, picked him up, asked each other if they were okay, hugged each other, then jumped around with joy. One of them yelled "Ready, set, go," and they all ran off together. It didn't matter who won but that they enjoyed the race together.

I don't call these people abnormal. This is how normality should be. We can learn something from these beautiful people. Dreams are individual, yet they are collective as well.

Heart Attack!

These are some of the qualities of a dreamer's heart which will help you pursue your dream. Another way to emphasise them is to look at the opposites, the areas we need to avoid. These kind of habits and principles will lead to a self-induced "heart attack". They include:

1. Lying.

Distort, twist, adjust or re-arrange the truth once and you'll probably do it again. And again. And you'll lose people's trust.

2. Manipulation.

Manipulation is dangerous–it is a sure fire way of losing the respect and trust of others. And if your actions are uncovered, it can take a long time to convince people you made a mistake and won't do it again. People are not objects to be pushed around.

3. Illicit Relationships

If there is one quick way to destroy your dreams and those of future generations, it is to be morally corrupt. Adultery is putting a knife to the throat of yourself and ripping the heart out of your family. Not only that, your peers and followers will lose all respect and admiration for you.

SUMMARY

THE HEART
1. Have a love for others
2. Be compassionate, not ruthless
3. Don't hold grudges
4. Contribute to others
5. Keep sweet
6. Don't carry hurts or bitterness
7. Forgive
8. Enjoy others' successes, don't be threatened by them

WAKE UP AND DREAM

9. Be honest
10. Never quit
11. Learn from hard times
12. Have faith
13. Don't walk over the top of others
14. Maintain high standards
15. Have good values
16. Accept yourself–you're unique
17. Be excited
18. Work together with others

Chapter Ten

THE STOMACH

An appetite for dreaming

Good food equals good health. Positive thoughts and input lead to positive thinking and a belief that you can attain your dreams.

You need to be careful what you "feed" yourself, because without the energy to maintain your progress, you'll fall short of the goal.

What's on a dreamer's menu? Positive books, tapes, videos, TV programs, discussion with fellow dreamers and so on. What's on the junk food list? Anything that can slow you down, de-motivate you, pull you down or, worse still, stop you. Maybe it's newspapers, magazines, TV, videos, critical friends?

We all have preconceived ideas, philosophies and traditions about life. They come from our upbringing. The trouble is many of these can slow us down. As dreamers we need to be "free flowing" and not "constipated" by small-minded thinking, traditional methods, hurts, fears or blockages from the past.

Consider this. We consume food to create energy and we use that energy to create a result. Input creates output. I am continually reading positive books and magazines and listening to cassettes, all by other dreamers, other "doers". To be a dreamer it's important to be digesting a constant flow of healthy "food".

A Solid Diet of Big Hearted Dreamers

Some of the most nourishing "food" for dreamers comes in the form of stories about other dreamers and their success. The world has seen some big-hearted dreamers. They are heroes to those of us pursuing our dreams. Their lives are testimonies that all things are possible to those who dream, plan and work with persistence and determination.

I could fill volumes with the great stories I've enjoyed and sought inspiration from. Here are some of the more prominent dreamers . . .

When **Henry Ford** wanted to produce a V8 engine his engineers all said it was impossible. "Produce it anyway," instructed the car magnate. "Stay on the job until you succeed, no matter how much time is required."

A year later they reported back to Henry with no breakthroughs. "Keep working. I want it and I'll have it." So the engineers went back to their drawing boards and, lo and behold, they finally worked it out. Ford released the V8 in his cars and became the most successful car manufacturer in the world.

It is said that it took eighteen years for Henry to build the motor car; today they can roll one off the production line in eighteen hours; and in the future we might be doing it in eighteen minutes. The car makers who have followed Henry have continued his dream.

"Whether you think you can or whether you think you can't, you're probably right."
Henry Ford

For years **Harland Sanders** worked hard to build a restaurant and motel business but was left penniless when the highway on which it was located was re-routed. He was forced to sell everything at auction just to cover his losses.

Rather than give up and retire on government handouts, Harland grabbed a pressure cooker and some of his now famous special seasoning and drove across America in an old Ford. He went from restaurant to restaurant frying up batches of chicken and asking chefs and owners to try his "finger lickin' good" recipe. He drove for many hundreds of kilometres before making his first sale.

That restaurant owner became the first of several hundred millionaires in the Kentucky Fried Chicken business and, as we know, Colonel Sanders became a very wealthy and famous man in the later years of his life.

McDonalds is one of the prime business success stories of our time. Today, the corporation is opening new outlets all over the world and turning over literally millions of dollars every day. Yet this food giant was once the dream of one man, **Ray Crock.**

---

*"All our dreams can come true
if we have the courage
to pursue them."*
Walt Disney

Ray was impressed with a hamburger outlet in Des Moines, Iowa, run by the McDonald brothers and became their partner. He came up with the idea of duplicating their shop to serve customers on the other side of town. Despite a lot of financial opposition from reluctant investors and the McDonalds (who he later bought out), he went ahead. Then he started outlets in other towns, and states, and countries. The rest is history.

Steven Spielberg has produced the award winning *Schindler's List, Jurassic Park* and such brilliant movies as *ET* and *Raiders of the Lost Ark*. When he was young he decided he wanted to be a movie producer. So he wangled his way onto movie sets and watched the professionals in action, then went home and tried to copy them with his Dad's old movie camera. He even found an abandoned caravan on one movie set and painted his name with a star on the door. He believed that one day he would be great. He was right.

In *Schindler's List*, the story of how the German entrepreneur Oscar Schindler saved many Jews in occupied Poland during World War II, we see the transformation of a man from shrewd businessman to selfless benefactor. Beginning as an opportunist exploiting Jews, we watch him change into someone who looks at his car and asks himself why he didn't sell it–the profit would have saved a few more lives. Eventually the film arrives at the scene where he is staring down the gun barrels of the Nazi soldiers and courageously challenging them to kill him now, or return home to their families and be real men. The impact of this movie has been felt around the world, and it all started from a dream in one man's heart.

I was reading a success book recently and it said that **Walt Disney**, the creator of Disneyland and the Disney characters, approached in the order of three hundred banks and financial institutions before he got the backing to build Disneyland. You don't have to tell me what an impact this one man has made on the world–I was raised on Goofy, Uncle Scrooge and Mickey. But would you have had the perseverance, the guts, to keep going back time and time again–Ignoring the rejection, Ignoring the "advice,"–Three hundred times?

Never Give Up

Now consider this. In 1832 a certain man lost his job. Despite this setback he decided to do something most people never even consider: he ran in a parliamentary election.

He failed to get the necessary votes.

Upon returning to the business world, he failed in business after just one year. He continued persistently to rebuild his business, but two years later tragedy struck–his sweetheart died. The following year, 1836, the pressure caused him to suffer a nervous breakdown.

This man had two options: to give up and accept that he was no good, or to keep on. He chose the latter.

Despite the breakdown, business failure and personal tragedy he continued to have great political aspirations.

In 1838 he ran in another election, for the role of parliamentary Speaker. He lost. Five years later he campaigned for the American Congress. He didn't have the numbers. In 1846 he again ran for Congress, and this time he succeeded–fourteen years after making his first attempt.

"Never give up,
never give up,
never, ever give up."
Winston Churchill

Victory, however, was short lived, for two years later he was defeated again. In 1849 he campaigned to return to Congress, but lost.

How many people would have kept on going?

This persistent dreamer did. Despite suffering the humiliation of more than twenty years of failure, five years later he launched another campaign–this time for a seat in the US Senate. He was defeated.

In 1856 he put his name down to become the next Vice-President of the United States. He lost. Again, in 1858, he campaigned to join the Senate. Again he was defeated.

Just two years later, this man with a huge dream that he never let go of was named the sixteenth President of the most powerful nation on earth. He was **Abraham Lincoln**, possibly the greatest leader the United States ever had.

Associate With Dreamers

Be very careful where you get your advice from. Certain people, even close friends, live in negativity. For them, being negative is the "norm". They tend to only see problems, never solutions. They suffer from Tall Poppy Syndrome, not wanting others to overtake them or outdo them. So they try to pull you back to their level.

Dreamers need to hang around other dreamers.

There's a story told of an old Chinese sage who was coming from a city. A young man approached him and asked, "My good friend, what is the city like where you have come from?"

The sage replied by asking the same question: "What is the city like where you have come from?" The young man described it as a place with dirty old buildings, dirty streets, bad weather and rude, unfriendly people. "The place you're headed for is much the same," said the sage.

A little while later another young man approached him from the same direction and asked, "What is the city like where you have come from?" The sage repeated the same question back to him. The young man described a beautiful place with kind, courteous people. "The place you're headed for is much the same."

Associate with dreamers, listen to them, read biographies of great dreamers. Be inspired by those who are doing the abnormal, and choose to be like them.

SUMMARY

THE STOMACH
1. Have a healthy diet–books, tapes, etc.
2. Stay away from junk food–negative magazines, newspapers, movies, critical friends

THE DIGESTIVE SYSTEM
1. Allow free flowing thoughts
2. Don't stifled by tradition or small mindedness
3. Digest books, tapes, magazines

Chapter Eleven

THE LEGS
AND FEET

Time for action

Legs and feet are built for distance because dreamers are marathon runners, not sprinters. If you'll pardon the expression, legs and feet are where the rubber hits the road! Without legs and feet you can't move on. But with them you can walk, run, hop, skip and jump!

I'd love to see you take the ideas from this book and turn them into action. A car won't go anywhere in neutral, but put it in Drive and it will. I'd love to see you get into gear and plant your foot. I'd love to see you put on your running shoes and explode out of the blocks!

If I decided to compete in the Olympics and take on the world record holder for the 1000 metres, I'd have to buy special running shoes. But if they stayed inside the box looking nice and clean that wouldn't improve my times. I would have to put them on and get them dirty and smelly.

The first day I started my training I would probably want to die–after just one run! I'm sure my feet would want to go into early retirement. Then on the second day I'd look to go a little faster, and my feet would probably hurt a little less. With each new day I'd be toughening them up. Less blisters, less pain, until the day I could match Carl Lewis' times and my feet would be supple and feeling good.

Dreaming is identical. It's possible to read motivational books, listen to self-development tapes, and do nothing. It's possible to dream the dreams yet never step out in faith and pursue them.

Perseverance Pays

I started off years ago leading a youth group, speaking to less than a hundred people at a time. How is it that today I speak to large gatherings of thousands? (I recently spoke to sixty eight thousand at one meeting.) The simple fact is if you stick at something long enough and you get good enough at it, people will recognise you for your achievements. I could never have achieved it in my first year, or second. But after fifteen years stickability, I've gained experience.

One of the greatest sermons ever given in the Bible is the Beatitudes. This is a list of principles which lead to blessing in life. "Blessed is he who . . ." Well, here's a beatitude of my own: Blessed are the doers, for they get things done!

The feet run *through* challenges rather than *from* them, sidestepping obstacles, out manoeuvring hindrances and leaping over temporary setbacks. And dreamers get back on their feet after being knocked down.

The depth of your character and the strength of your dream determines how long you will stick it out.

There will always be obstacles in life, and there will always be obstacles between you and your dream. Treat them as temporary setbacks and nuisances. In many cases, a negative can become a positive learning, evaluating and fine-tuning process—rather than a killer of the dream.

For example, if you are on your way to building a successful business and your most important right hand person leaves you, you can do one of three things. You can crumble and give up altogether. You can take on the work yourself. Or you can begin a strategy to train up someone else to take on that role.

I would suggest that you approach such an occurrence as a temporary hiccup with long-term benefits. Train up a new person the way you want them to be, with the loyalty you want them to have. Share and instil your dream into them, and allow them expression and creativity in their new role.

Rather than allowing circumstances to affect you, you can take control.

I like the words of former British Prime Minister Winston Churchill on this: *"One ought never to turn one's back on a threatened danger and try to run away from it. If you do that you will double the danger. But if you meet it promptly and without flinching you will reduce the danger by half. Never run away from anything."*

A Dreamer's Legs Go Anywhere

Talking about legs makes me think of a great dreamer who used his in a way that made the whole world sit up and take notice. No, not Carl Lewis or Ben Johnson. It was an English high school graduate, Robert Swan.

Recognising that his life wasn't really taking him anywhere, Robert became fascinated with a personal dream: to walk to the South Pole in the footsteps of the ill-fated explorer Captain Robert Scott! Not a bad dream for an eighteen-year-old who had absolutely no knowledge of ice, snow, or expeditions.

For ten years he worked as a labourer, waiter and gardener to raise funds, and knocked on many many doors seeking sponsorship. Eventually Robert formed a team. He was the youngest and least experienced, but that didn't deter him. They took off for Antarctica and seventy-one days and 1413 kilometres later Robert Swan realised his childhood dream.

If you only walk when the sun shines, you'll never complete your journey.

However, the euphoria was short-lived. Their ship sank and the expedition put him in debt. To keep faith with his financial backers, Robert made a decision to travel round the world doing interviews, showing films and slides. Bit by bit he raised the necessary funds.

You'd think that the extreme weather conditions and mammoth challenges of one such "walkathon" would have been enough, even for the biggest dreamer. But it wasn't. Later, in 1989, the world news reported the fact that Robert Swan had completed a second treacherous journey by foot. To the North Pole!

Some years ago at Youth Alive, we "hit a wall". It was crisis time and to be honest with you, it was very emotionally draining. However what began as a major concern actually turned out to be our greatest triumph, because it caused us to re-adjust what we were doing. We built a stronger team, as we identified and ran with our strengths and worked on our weaknesses.

The Pain Of It All

The character of a person is measured by how they handle opposition. Opposition is a wonderful thing–if you enjoy pain! Opposition comes in all shapes and sizes. Some hindrances are harder to face than others. Some have answers that are quite simple, while others are not as easy to solve. Some never have happy endings.

When I think of hindrances I think of one of the great hymn writers, Horatio G. Spafford. He was a successful businessman in Chicago in the 1800s. He decided to sell everything he had to become a missionary and go and help the lost and hurting in the Middle East. His family set sail first whilst he stayed back to tend to final business arrangements.

During the voyage tragedy struck and everyone on the ship died, except one–his wife.

Horatio received a telegram and was told of the horror. Despite this terrible personal sadness, he didn't back down or compromise. He brought his wife back to America, packed his bags, and they left for the other side of the world together.

When they got to a particular point of the journey the captain said, "Mr Spafford, this is the exact location where your children and the others perished."

The pain of it all must have ripped his heart out. I'm a Dad and I know how much it hurts me if one of my children suffers harm. Yet, notwithstanding this, Horatio went below decks to his cabin and wrote these words:

When peace like a river attendeth my way,
When sorrows like sea billows roll;
Whatever my lot you have taught me to say:
"It is well, it is well with my soul!"

The desire to serve was not deterred by tragedy and out of that tragedy Horatio Spafford wrote one of the greatest songs of comfort and meaning that has ever been penned. It has comforted the anguished hearts of thousands for over a century.

How To Meet Challenges

I can't count the number of hindrances, obstacles and challenges I have had to face since I first took over those youth rallies. I have learnt over the years to approach them in a systematic way. I suggest that you adopt this simple technique I have learnt to use:

1. Don't freak out

Yelling, getting angry, pounding the desk, tearing your hair out or slamming doors doesn't solve anything. It only means you have a sore throat, sore hand, sore head and broken door.

You can't define anything in a state of confusion or emotional instability. It only blurs your vision.

2. Define the opposition

Do this by yourself or with the help of a "think tank". Often people outside your situation can be more objective than you because they are "outside looking in".

A problem well-defined is a problem half solved. If the problem is management, then look at it from that perspective. If it is strategy, then re-strategise.

Sometimes the obstacle to your dream might be an emotional one. It is important to seek counsel when facing an emotive situation and I suggest that you only seek counsel from men and women of character, not easy-fix "hotshots" without character or integrity. If it is a moral decision always choose the right way, the ethical way. Don't take the easy way out. Make decisions based on what is known to be morally and ethically correct in the eyes of society and the law. The hardest person to live with is your conscience. If you dull your conscience by making bad decisions, you will regret it in the long run.

3. Ask why

Often we just want to know how to get out of a situation, so we ask, "How do we get out of it?" But we fail to ask, "How did we get there in the first place?" Unless you ask why, there's a chance you will end up there again. This requires being honest with yourself and admitting your limitations or weaknesses, but it's worth it.

4. Develop a plan

Once you've clearly defined the obstacle, develop a strategy for overcoming it. In doing this, focus on the achievable.

5. Implement the changes

Take action. Don't let things drift and don't just talk. Treat challenges as an opportunity to move on positively.

SUMMARY

THE LEGS AND FEET
1. Support others
2. Life is a marathon not a sprint
3. Run through/over obstacles
4. Get things done
5. Crisis builds character
6. Don't panic
7. Define the opposition
8. Make morally right decisions
9. Ask why it occurred
10. Develop a plan
11. Implement changes
12. Stickability

PART THREE

FULFIL YOUR DESTINY

Chapter Twelve

HOW TO FIND
YOUR DREAM

WAKE UP AND DREAM

After World War II more than two hundred Frenchmen returned to Paris suffering from amnesia. They had been tortured in prisoner-of-war camps to such an extent that they couldn't remember who they were. Medical records and other information were used to establish the identities of all but 32.

Photos of the remaining people were published on the front pages of newspapers throughout the country and next-of-kin were asked to assemble in Paris on a particular day. The first of the amnesia victims walked out before the hushed crowd and pleadingly asked, "Does anybody out there know who I am?"

He asked the question out loud. For most of us the question is kept in our hearts. Find out your destiny, your life purpose, and fulfil it.

Be Yourself

Work on the inside, the inner qualities of your life.

Don't play a role that isn't you, don't live in a world of fantasy. You shouldn't be afraid to show who you really are. One of the reasons we don't want to do this is because we don't like what we see. However, if you put up a facade, it will only be a matter of time before people find out.

Accept yourself as you are. After all, if you're not you, how can you fulfil your dreams being somebody else?

Where Do I Find My Dream?

Ask yourself, "What am I good at? What do I want to do? Who do I want to be? How can I contribute to society? What difference can I make?" This is the first step.

Next, ask: "What is it that really gets me excited?" What stirs you, stimulates you, fires you up? Some people have a knack for making money, others are creative or technical, while others have an ability to be benevolent and charitable. There are leaders, facilitators, organisers, administrators. If you give me an audience of at least one, I can talk–it just comes out of me–though to get better at it takes a lifetime. Take a good look at yourself.

What comes easily?

Having identified your strengths, your natural abilities, take a look at what are your most productive areas. You will need to concentrate on these talents–not necessarily the ones you like best.

---

*If you don't have a dream,
find a need and fill it.*

And remember, persistence is the key. Some people start out with a roar but slow down and eventually stop with a whimper. Going halfway is not all the way. You are a marathon runner, not a sprinter.

Be A Chatterbox

Once you've got a dream, speak it into existence. As we saw in Chapter 6, words are very powerful. *"Life and death are in the power of the tongue"*, says the Bible. Begin telling yourself you don't feel good and you won't feel good. Tell yourself that your business is in a mess and it will get in a mess. Words have the ability to inspire, create, motivate, change.

Talk about your dream every day. Continually remind yourself of it. Think about it. Be on the lookout for opportunities. During this process it's very likely that you'll also make improvements to your dream because you'll be exposed to new and better ideas. The more you imagine your dream fulfilled, the more realistic it will become, the bigger and stronger it will become. Be a creative thinker: someone who is looking for positives, not obstacles. If you come up with feasible ideas make a note of them. They might seem premature now, but it's possible they will help you in the future.

As Napoleon said: "Imagination rules the world".

Leaders And Friends

Whether you're in the corporate field, ministry, volunteer work or a people-oriented area like network marketing, your strength (and weakness) will be in your leadership. No person is an expert at everything, and the sign of a good leader is someone who gathers about them a team of highly qualified people to assist them.

Build others up and release their giftings and talents. Inspire them, learn from them, set challenges for them and help them.

From the moment we are born to the day we die, our lives are about relationships. Relationships don't just happen, they are made.

WAKE UP AND DREAM

We live in a society which prides itself on high technology, free thinking and advancements in education and knowledge, yet we have one of the most despairing, drug dependent cultures ever known. Why? Because people aren't investing in relationships.

Friendship-building is vital.

Crash and Burn

Some people let their dreams destroy them. They go through burnout–nervous and physical exhaustion–in the pursuit of their goals. Your dream will die unless it is fun.

People don't burnout from what they enjoy. They get exhausted when they place themselves under incredible pressure or attempt things they aren't skilled at– generally things that are not part of the dream.

A brilliant movie which portrayed a business person living under immense pressure, and being unable to enjoy life and the pursuit of success, was *Hook*, with Robin Williams as Peter Pan.

Peter has left Never Never Land, grown up, and become a successful businessman. But in doing so he has lost his identity. Consequently his relationship with his son is non-existent and his family fights and argues. Hook invades his home, kidnaps his kids and Peter begins his quest, only to discover that he is Peter Pan. As he learns to play and be childlike again, he finds his identity and regains the love and affection of his family.

So often we take ourselves too seriously. One of the greatest keys to having a dream become reality is to enjoy life.

Have a rich sense of humour. Laugh a lot. You might consider this a strange statement, but the Bible says: "A merry heart does good like a medicine." Doctors have found direct links between good health and laughter and fun. Laugh at adversity, laugh as you go through challenges, look past tragedy.

What about horrific situations when you lose a loved one or face bankruptcy? Of course, these circumstances are full of pain and suffering but deep down inside every human being there is a capacity to break through. It's an attitude.

I Believe!

Fear and faith require the same input–belief–but their outworkings are very different. Faith is what you believe will happen; fear is also what you believe will happen. But faith is positive and fear is negative.

Faith is directly related to what I consider to be one of the most ignored aspects of life–our spirituality.

I have found that faith in God has given me values to base my dreams on and incredible inspiration and creativity. I've heard the comment over the years when talking to people that God wants to take things off you. In fact, He wants to add to your life. His desire is for you to live an abundant life–full of purpose, blessing, prosperity and success. My faith has given me a life purpose.

Our inner life makes us
what we are.
Everything else–the outward
- is superficial.

Whatever your spiritual persuasions, this aspect of your life shouldn't be overlooked or treated casually. As I mentioned earlier, true success means having balance in all areas and that includes your spirit life.

Wake Up The Dreamer

The greatest achievers are dreamers, and you can be one of them. At first it will seem like a daunting task–every bit as daunting as getting your body in condition if you're overweight and flabby. But just as you can achieve muscle tone, fitness and strength by working on it, so you can fulfil your dreams one step at a time. Work on each little area and watch yourself move closer and closer to your dream.

That's how I've tackled it. As I now look forward to holding Youth Alive rallies in forty thousand seat football stadiums around the world and impacting more people to become a future generation we can be proud of, I'm facing the challenges one step at a time.

You don't have to be just a part of history–you can help forge it!

Wake up the dreamer inside you and *GO FOR IT!*

SUMMARY

1. Know who you are: be yourself
2. Work on your inner qualities
3. If you don't have a dream, find a need and fill it
4. Identify your strengths
5. Speak your dream into existence
6. Develop other people
7. Have fun
8. Choose faith, not fear
9. Keep your dream alive and GO FOR IT!

Chapter Thirteen

THE LEGACY OF A DREAMER

When you eventually farewell this planet you will leave behind a legacy. Friends and family will have certain memories about who you were. It's up to you whether you'll leave a legacy of joy, happiness, good character and pride, or a legacy of unhappiness, failure and tragedy.

The kind of work you do will reflect the kind of person you are. I want to leave an indelible mark on the young people that I come in contact with. I want to inspire them to missionary service, to excellence, to be generous to be part of the answer not part of the problem.

Leaving An Inheritance

If you, like me, are a parent, have you ever considered leaving an inheritance for your children? Your childrens' children? Have you thought of pursuing something which will have a positive effect on future generations? Most people live in the here and now, but we need to have long-range thinking.

A brilliant example of this is seen in the life of Jim Henson, of *Sesame Street* and Muppet fame. Sadly, Jim died in 1990 from a severe bout of pneumonia and the world farewelled a great dreamer.

Born in 1936, Jim was the kid picked last for baseball or football teams. He preferred to spend his time daydreaming or watching puppets on his family's new television. He joined a high school puppet club which led to a job with a TV station and a five-minute late-night show with his first creation–Kermit.

Convinced the Muppets were a great vehicle for a family series, he went to the American television networks, but they turned him down. It took twenty years to attract the support he needed–and when it came it wasn't from his native America. England's Lord Grade helped expose the world to *The Muppet Show*.

Jim pushed himself hard. More than two thousand puppets were created over the years. By the late 1980s *Sesame Street* was being watched by nearly three-quarters of all American households with little children, and *The Muppet Show* was being screened weekly to two hundred and thirty five million viewers in more than a hundred countries. Jim Henson Productions received 22 Emmys.

Jim's close friend and assistant puppeteer,

Frank Oz, said: "Jim the creator was a genius. Yet I see Jim foremost as an appreciator. He appreciated the Muppet family and his own family. He appreciated flying kites with his children. He appreciated beauty, and he appreciated fun."

What a fantastic way to be remembered. And let's face it, every time we see *Sesame Street* on TV or Big Bird or Oscar in the toy department we're seeing part of the legacy of one man's dream.

Today, Jim's son Brian continues the vision as a puppeteer in his own right. The dreamer might die but the dream doesn't. Or, as said before: *"There's something greater than money. It's called purpose."*

"There is no royal road to anything.
One thing at a time,
all things in succession.
That which grows fast,
withers as rapidly.
That which grows
slowly, endures."
Josiah Gilbert Holland

WAKE UP AND DREAM

The Decade of Dreams

I look back on the 1960s as a remarkable time. From our current point in history, it seems the 1960s was a time of big dreamers.

I was reminded of this during a flight one day. There I was, taking off for yet another speaking engagement. I struggled onto the plane with my "essentials"–a carry bag ready to burst open and two giant suitcases full of tapes and books–and forced my way down the narrow aisle. I found my seat, stowed my luggage (no small feat), sat down to regain my strength and enjoyed a nice cold orange juice.

Then came the bad news. The plane was grounded due to mechanical failure. I dragged the bags out of the storage lockers, grabbed my heavy load and made my way past the seats. Bang, thump, bang, thump.

A second plane was waiting not far away. I again defied the laws of physics by squeezing my bags into the locker, then relaxed. The movie screen lit up and the aircraft cabin resounded to the amazing sounds of a bygone era. Onto the screen leapt Peter, Paul and Mary in concert.

I quickly forgot about my aching shoulders and departure delays. The folk trio began to sing songs of hope, songs filled with dreams, songs of answers about a generation of dreamers. I saw parents holding their children and singing *If I Had A Hammer, Puff The Magic Dragon* and other songs with motivating lyrics.

As I watched, I began to think of our world today and one of the greatest tragedies that has ever happened. We have lost the ability to dream.

"To cease to think creatively
is but little different f
rom ceasing to live."
Ben Franklin

I know the 1960s was a time of confusion and disillusionment. It saw the start of drug experimentation and free sex cultures. It saw the start of a long bitter war. It saw the the rock 'n' roll phenomena take off. But in the midst of all of this there were brilliant people willing to step forward and be counted. Really big dreamers like preacher and civil rights leader Martin Luther King and US President John F. Kennedy.

King radically changed a nation's culture. I've read his famous "I have a dream . . . " speech. Talk about dreams! This guy had an enormous vision for the future, and he was willing to do anything to see it come to pass.

You'll pick up some of that determination and vision in this excerpt of the speech, where he verbalises his life goal:

"I have a dream that one day this nation will rise up and live out the true meaning of its creed: 'We hold these truths to be self-evident that all men are created equal.' I have a dream that one day on the red hills of Georgia sons of former slaves and the sons of former slave own-ers will be able to sit down together at the table of brotherhood. I have a dream that my four little children will one day live in a nation where they will not be judged by the colour of their skin but by the content of their character ..."

I was reading a magazine about the Kennedys recently. It said when John was just a small boy attending primary school his mother told him she believed he would be the first Irish Catholic President of the United States. She repeated this dream over and over, speaking it into his life. The dream came to pass and J. F. Kennedy brought vision and hope to America. Without his enthusiasm and faith we wouldn't have landed on the moon.

Tragically, these "super-dreamers" were assassinated. Yet, both left behind powerful legacies. To this day they remain champions of change–examples of *"The Power of One"* (if I can borrow that movie title).

WAKE UP AND DREAM

Is The Dream Over?

Rock legend Mick Jagger stated at the end of the 1960s, "The dream is over". In a way, he was right. As I think back over the 1970s and 1980s, I don't recall the same fervour and visionary zeal of that earlier period in time. The 1990s have witnessed isolated incidents, such as Nelson Mandela's vision to bring equality to South Africa. But they are still dubbed the Nervous Nineties because this generation is the first to be raised in the Nuclear Age without a potential future.

The people of the Hi-tech Age are a people robbed of some of their spontaneity, imagination and individuality. They're also the first generation to face the full exposure of the media. The current generation is seeing widespread moral breakdown. The "baby boomers" listened to the Beatles and Rolling Stones and watched *The Brady Bunch*. Today's young people listen to Sodom, Sleeping Dead and Madonna and watch *The Simpsons*. With some countries seeing more than one in three marriages end in divorce, the family unit is under attack. Values have become twisted. There is no longer a clear right and wrong.

Society wants moral, ethical leaders and dreamers to stand up and point the way ahead. Where are they?

What A Dreamer!

One person who I believe will leave behind an incredible legacy is Mother Teresa. What a dreamer! What an achiever! Who can guess how many lives she has touched in her lifetime?

One of my favourite illustrations of her courage and single minded attitude happened after she had spoken to the United Nations in New York. She decided to visit a maximum security prison not far away and ended up speaking to four inmates with AIDS. They brought back memories of the lepers she had been helping in her native Calcutta.

Mother Teresa was spurred into action. It was the Monday before Christmas, but all the same she went straight to the Mayor of New York and asked him to contact the governor, Mario Cuomo.

"Governor," she said over the phone, "I'm just back from Sing Sing and four prisoners there have AIDS. I'd like to open up an AIDS centre. Would you mind releasing those four prisoners to me? I'd like them to be the first four in the AIDS centre."

"We have 43 cases of AIDS in the state prison system," replied Cuomo. "I'll release all 43 to you."

"I'd like to start with just the four. Now let me tell you about the building I have in mind.

Would you like to pay for it?"

The governor was bowled over by her intensity and agreed. Mother Teresa then turned to the Mayor and stated, "Today is Monday. I'd like to open this on Wednesday. We're going to need some permits cleared. Could you please arrange those?"

What fierce determination!

It doesn't matter what title you have... what matters is what you leave behind.

I'm sure the legacies of the Abraham Lincolns, George Washingtons, J.F. Kennedys and Mother Teresas'–will be remembered for all time. The legacy of the founder of the Salvation Army, William Booth, is still felt today all over world, as this conquering army helps to defeat devastation, disease, poverty and sickness. Booth's dream lives on bigger than he ever imagined.

The challenge to us is that our dreams out-live us. It doesn't matter what title you have–what matters is what you leave behind.

So dream on, baby, dream on!

Chapter Fourteen

THE DREAMER'S CHECKLIST

WAKE UP AND DREAM

Run through this Dreamer's Checklist and start building your plan of action today!

You need dreams in your life to ...

- [ ] Better yourself
- [ ] Give your life purpose and direction
- [ ] Not be controlled by outside circumstances
- [ ] Get out of existence mode
- [ ] Get more enjoyment out of life
- [ ] Affect other people's lives for the better

PART ONE–WAKE UP

- [ ] Determine to Wake Up
- [ ] Declare war on apathy, compromise and procrastination
- [ ] Consider your purpose in life
- [ ] Analyse your abilities and talents
- [ ] Don't wait for a "big break"–conceive your dream now
- [ ] Nurture your dream through its "pregnancy"
- [ ] Be willing to endure the pain of "birthing" your dream
- [ ] Allow your dream to grow in stages
- [ ] Think big–your "infant" dream will bear little resemblance to your "mature" dream

PART TWO–DEVELOP YOUR DREAMER'S ANATOMY

Head and Mind

- ☐ Don't be superficial or build a facade
- ☐ Seek inner qualities such as honesty, integrity and truth
- ☐ Think positively
- ☐ Become solution-oriented
- ☐ Become a creative thinker
- ☐ Use your imagination
- ☐ Choose your moods, attitudes and responses
- ☐ Think BIG!!!

The Eyes

- ☐ See beyond circumstances
- ☐ See the future; know where you're going
- ☐ Be single focussed, not distracted
- ☐ If you can't do everything you want, select the most important areas

The Ears

- ☐ Become an active listener
- ☐ Have empathy and genuine concern
- ☐ Listen for the "inner cry"

WAKE UP AND DREAM

The Tongue

- [ ] Speak encouragement be positive
- [ ] Choose your words wisely
- [ ] Be trustworthy; keep confidences
- [ ] Communicate your dream
- [ ] Affirm the dream
- [ ] Repeat the dream
- [ ] Impart the dream
- [ ] Write the dream down
- [ ] Repeat the dream over and over out loud (use cards)
- [ ] Own your dream
- [ ] Talk about it daily

The Backbone

- [ ] Plan for your dream
- [ ] Turn dream into goals–years, months, weeks
- [ ] Make goals S.M.A.R.T.
    - Specific
    - Measurable
    - Action oriented
    - Realistic
    - Timetabled
- [ ] Use a day planner
- [ ] Pace yourself
- [ ] Let your plans be flexible
- [ ] Don't over-plan
- [ ] Seek balance in all areas of life

- ☐ Value family and relationships
- ☐ Be accountable

The Hands

- ☐ Embrace other people
- ☐ Work hard
- ☐ Link hands with other dreamers
- ☐ Don't point the finger; don't judge others
- ☐ Write down your vision
- ☐ Keep it simple
- ☐ Find faithful people to work with
- ☐ Be approachable

The Heart

- ☐ Have love for others
- ☐ Be compassionate, not ruthless
- ☐ Don't hold grudges
- ☐ Contribute to the lives of others
- ☐ Keep sweet
- ☐ Don't carry hurts or bitterness
- ☐ Forgive and forget
- ☐ Enjoy others' successes; don't be threatened by them
- ☐ Be honest
- ☐ Never quit
- ☐ Learn from hard times
- ☐ Have faith
- ☐ Don't walk over the top of others
- ☐ Maintain high standards and values

WAKE UP AND DREAM

- ☐ Accept yourself–you're unique
- ☐ Be excited
- ☐ Work together with others

The Stomach

- ☐ Maintain a healthy diet–books, tapes, etc.
- ☐ Stay away from junk food–negative magazines, newspapers, movies, critical friends
- ☐ Keep to free flowing thoughts–not stifled by tradition or small mindedness

The Legs and Feet

- ☐ Support others
- ☐ Life is a marathon, not a sprint–pace yourself
- ☐ Run through obstacles and crash through the barriers–crisis builds character
- ☐ Get things done
- ☐ Don't panic
- ☐ Define the opposition
- ☐ Implement changes
- ☐ Develop your endurance and stickability

PART THREE–FULFIL YOUR DESTINY

- [ ] Know who you are
- [ ] Work on your inner qualities
- [ ] Be patient–the dream takes time
- [ ] Be friendly, not aloof
- [ ] Be careful where your advice comes from
- [ ] Associate with dreamers
- [ ] Find a need and fill it (if you don't have a dream)
- [ ] Identify your strengths
- [ ] Have fun
- [ ] Keep the dream alive
- [ ] Develop other people
- [ ] Have belief

WAKE UP AND DREAM

WAKE UP AND DREAM

Pat Mesiti's ministry and international speaking career provide you with valuable resources that will empower you to achieve greater success in life.

If *Wake Up and Dream* has helped you to discover your dream and unlock your potential then place your order for Pat's other outstanding tapes and books ... valuable aids to you and your family's future.

Tapes

Building Big People _____ 2 tape set
Super Success Strategies _____ 3 tape set
Vision, Values & Destiny _____ 4 tape set
Wake Up and Dream _____ 3 tape set
Sowing and Reaping _____ 3 tape set

Books

It's Only Rock and Roll, but ...

For more information on products by Pat Mesiti complete the order form over the page or contact:

Pat Mesiti Ministries
P O Box 1165 Castle Hill NSW 2154 Australia
Tel: Int + 612 899 6713 or Int + 612 634 7633
Fax: Int + 612 899 3740

WAKE UP AND DREAM

Please rush me the following tapes and books ...

- ☐ *Building Big People* _____ $20
- ☐ *Super Success Strategies* _____ $25
- ☐ *Vision, Values & Destiny* _____ $30
- ☐ *Wake Up and Dream* _____ $25
- ☐ *Sowing and Reaping* _____ $25
- ☐ *It's Only Rock and Roll, but ...* _____ $10

Plus $5.00 postage **TOTAL VALUE** $AUS _____

Name _____

Address _____

_____

Phone (_____) _____

Fax (_____) _____

Please debit my credit card to the value of $AUS _____

TYPE OF CARD ☐ MasterCard ☐ Visa ☐ Bankcard

☐☐☐☐☐☐☐☐☐☐☐☐☐☐☐☐☐☐☐☐☐☐

Card Number

Expiry Date _____

Signature _____

PHONE, FAX OR MAIL YOUR ORDER TODAY TO ...

Pat Mesiti Ministries
P O Box 1165 Castle Hill NSW 2154 Australia
Tel: Int + 612 899 6713 or Int + 612 634 7633
Fax: Int + 612 899 3740